8/50

The Honourable
Gordon F. Osbaldeston
P.C., O.C.

KEEPING
DEPUTY
MINISTERS
ACCOUNTABLE

The Honourable
Gordon F. Osbaldeston
P.C., O.C.

Keeping
Deputy
Ministers
Accountable

McGRAW-HILL RYERSON
Toronto Montreal

KEEPING DEPUTY MINISTERS ACCOUNTABLE

First published in 1989 by
McGraw-Hill Ryerson Limited
330 Progress Avenue
Scarborough, Ontario M1P 2Z5

ISBN 0-07-549794-8
1 2 3 4 5 6 7 8 9 0 M 8 7 6 5 4 3 2 1 0 9

National Centre for Management
Research and Development
University of Western Ontario
London, Ontario, Canada N6A 3K7
(519) 661-3233

Printed and bound in Canada

Canadian Cataloguing in Publication Data

Osbaldeston, Gordon F.
  Keeping deputy ministers accountable

Includes bibliographical references.
ISBN 0-07-549794-8

1. Administrative responsibility — Canada.
2. Canada — Executive departments. 3. Government executives — Canada. 4. Canada — Officials and employees. I. Title.

JL111.E93026 1988   354.71009'9   C88-095408-6

To my wife Gerry, whose constructive criticism and constant support have shaped both the substance and values underlying this report, and my career.

Contents

PREFACE
ACKNOWLEDGEMENTS

CHAPTER **1 INTRODUCTION**   1

    1.1 RESEARCH APPROACH   3
    1.2 DEFINITIONS: ACCOUNTABILITY,
       MANAGEMENT RESPONSIBILITY AND
       ANSWERABILITY   5
    1.3 OVERVIEW: THE ACCOUNTABILITY
       SYSTEM OF DEPUTY MINISTERS   6

CHAPTER **2 ACCOUNTABILITY OF DEPUTY
MINISTERS TO MINISTERS**   11

    2.1 THE ROLE OF THE MINISTER   11
    2.2 THE ROLE OF THE DEPUTY MINISTER   15
    2.3 THE MINISTER-DEPUTY MINISTER TEAM   22
    2.4 MAKING THE TEAM WORK: THE
       IMPORTANCE OF TRUST   25
    2.5 CHIEF POLITICAL AIDES: POLITICAL
       AND PARTISAN SUPPORT   38
    2.6 MINISTERS OF STATE: ADDED
       COMPLEXITY   44
    2.7 THE DEPUTY MINISTER'S ANSWER-
       ABILITY TO PARLIAMENT   46
    2.8 FINDINGS: ACCOUNTABILITY OF
       DEPUTY MINISTERS TO MINISTERS   49

CHAPTER **3 ACCOUNTABILITY OF DEPUTY
MINISTERS TO THE PRIME MINISTER
AND CENTRAL AGENCIES**   51

    3.1 MINISTER AND DEPUTY MINISTER:
       DIVISION OF COLLECTIVE MANAGE-
       MENT RESPONSIBILITIES   52
    3.2 THE DEPUTY MINISTER'S
       ACCOUNTABILITY TO THE PRIME
       MINISTER   53

3.3 THE DEPUTY MINISTER'S
ACCOUNTABILITY TO THE PUBLIC
SERVICE COMMISSION   60

3.4 THE DEPUTY MINISTER'S
ACCOUNTABILITY TO THE TREASURY
BOARD   64

3.5 MANAGING THE COMPLEXITY: THE
INFORMAL SYSTEM   69

3.6 LIMITS TO ACCOUNTABILITY FOR
COLLECTIVE MANAGEMENT   72

3.7 RECENT REFORMS: INCREASING
DEPARTMENT ACCOUNTABILITY AND
RESPONSIBILITY   76

3.8 FINDINGS: ACCOUNTABILITY FOR
COLLECTIVE MANAGEMENT   79

CHAPTER 4 MANAGING THE MINISTER'S AGENDA   81

4.1 THE AGENDA-SETTING ENVIRONMENT   81
4.2 THE MINISTER'S AGENDA   87
4.3 THE ROLE OF THE DEPUTY MINISTER
IN SETTING THE MINISTER'S AGENDA   92
4.4 IMPLEMENTING THE MINISTER'S
AGENDA   96
4.5 FINDINGS: MANAGING THE
MINISTER'S AGENDA   105

CHAPTER 5 MANAGING THE DEPARTMENT   107

5.1 TAKING CHARGE OF A DEPARTMENT   108
5.2 THE LEADERSHIP CHALLENGE   119
5.3 THE CHANGING MANAGEMENT
NEEDS OF A DEPARTMENT   129
5.4 ACCOUNTABILITY IN THE PRIVATE
SECTOR   132
5.5 FINDINGS: DEPARTMENT
MANAGEMENT   136

CHAPTER 6 MANAGING THE DEPUTY MINISTER
GROUP   139

6.1 JUST PASSING THROUGH: TENURE OF
DEPUTY MINISTERS   139

6.2 DEVELOPMENT AND TENURE OF
CHIEF EXECUTIVE OFFICERS   149
6.3 ASSESSMENT OF DEPUTY MINISTER
PERFORMANCE   152
6.4 PERSONAL VALUES: THE PUBLIC
SERVICE ETHIC   156
6.5 WHERE WILL THE NEXT GENERATION
OF DEPUTY MINISTERS COME FROM?   158
6.6 FINDINGS: MANAGING THE DEPUTY
MINISTER GROUP   159

CHAPTER 7 **CONCLUSIONS AND
RECOMMENDATIONS**   161

7.1 CONCLUSIONS   162
7.2 RECOMMENDATIONS   167

CASES

EARNING THE MINISTER'S CONFIDENCE   28
THE POLICY ADVICE CASE   32
MANAGING THE POLICY PROCESS   34
THE VEHICLE SAFETY CASE   35
THE REGIONAL DEVELOPMENT CASE   98
THE MANDATE CASE   100
THE RESOURCE CASE   102
THE ENFORCEMENT CASE   115
THE DEPARTMENT DOWNSIZING CASE   124

FIGURES

FIGURE 1-1 ACCOUNTABILITY OF THE
DEPUTY MINISTER   8
FIGURE 2-1 THE DEPUTY MINISTER'S
MANAGEMENT ENVIRONMENT   16
FIGURE 4-1 THE GOVERNMENT AGENDA-
SETTING PROCESS   83
FIGURE 4-2 THE MINISTER'S AGENDA-
SETTING PROCESS   85
FIGURE 5-1 DEPARTMENT MANAGEMENT
REQUIREMENTS   112

FIGURE 6-1 AVERAGE DEPUTY MINISTER
TENURE: 1960-1987   141
FIGURE 6-2 DEPUTY MINISTERS WITH MORE
THAN 3 YEARS IN THE
DEPARTMENT: 1960-1987   142
FIGURE 6-3 DEPUTY MINISTERS WITH MORE
THAN 5 YEARS' EXPERIENCE:
1960-1987   143
FIGURE 6-4 MINISTER-DEPUTY MINISTER
TEAM TENURE: 1960-1987   144

NOTES   187

PREFACE

When Gordon Osbaldeston joined the faculty of the School of Business Administration at the University of Western Ontario, I asked him to consider doing some research on management in the public sector through the National Centre for Management Research and Development (NCMRD). As a result, he brought forward a major research proposal, arranged for outside financing, built a research team, and has now come forward with what I believe is a path-breaking piece of research. I am proud to be associated with this study on the accountability of deputy ministers, and NCMRD is very pleased to be able to publish it.

From the point of view of NCMRD, this study represented a rare opportunity to bring together three major sources of information that could further the understanding of management and accountability in the public sector. We were particularly interested in combining the unique experience of a former deputy minister and Secretary to the Cabinet; the insights and perceptions of a wide range of ministers and deputy ministers about government; and the advanced concepts and literature that have been developed in the private sector for analysing the roles of managers and understanding how complex organizations work.

The mission of the NCMRD is to develop research and information that can help public and private organizations improve their managerial performance. This research and final report provide an insightful understanding of how deputy ministers work within the context of the federal government. It has also helped to provide a valuable bridge for business people and business schools to better understand the realities of managing in the public sector.

To ensure that this research was methodologically sound and took advantage of current management thinking and literature, the NCMRD appointed an advisory group of professors from the School of Business Administration. This group, composed of Jim Hatch, Harry Lane and Rod White, was consulted on several occasions throughout the study. The response to the methodology and results by the advisory group, other faculty members, and the Board of Directors of the NCMRD, was extremely positive and helpful to the researchers.

This study has opened up important new concepts and frontiers for research in the field of public sector management. It has illustrated the importance of understanding the unique characteristics of the public sector environment and the importance of appreciating the challenges that governments face. It has shown that private sector concepts and literature have distinct limitations in providing prescriptions for management and accountability in government. At the same time, it has drawn on modern management literature to develop a perceptive understanding of the roles of deputy ministers and how they work in a complex and uncertain environment.

A key part of the mandate of NCMRD is to disseminate research findings so that managers are able to use them to advantage. I am very pleased that Gordon Osbaldeston has agreed to continue working in this area and will be available to discuss this report with various groups across the country.

David S.R. Leighton
Director
National Centre for Management
Research and Development

ACKNOWLEDGEMENTS

This study could not have been done without the support and participation of many different individuals and groups. First, I want to thank the Honourable Erik Nielsen who asked me to undertake this independent study when he was deputy prime minister. I have a great admiration for the work he did in reviewing program expenditures in the federal government. This study aims to further his work by illustrating some of the requirements for keeping deputy ministers accountable.

The work of this study was made possible by the support and funding of C.B. Johnston, Dean, School of Business Administration and David Leighton, Director, National Centre for Management Research and Development (NCMRD). NCMRD has not only provided me with financial support to do this work, but has been a major source of advice and encouragement. It has been very heartening to find a genuine interest in public sector management issues among my colleagues at NCMRD and the School of Business at the University of Western Ontario.

The research for this study was also supported in various ways by the Business Council on National Issues (BCNI), the Institute for Research on Public Policy (IRPP), the Conference Board of Canada and Max Bell Foundation. The support of these private agencies enabled us to complement our research program with some vital work with respect to Parliament and the private sector.

The federal government also contributed significantly to this study. First of all, I was very fortunate to be able to recruit Richard Paton, then with the Office of the Auditor General and now with the Privy Council Office, as my Executive Director. Richard was the architect of the research program and was responsible for managing the study team as well as drafting speeches and presentations and preparing the final report. Richard managed a complex, innovative research program which drew upon the experience and insights of deputy ministers. His ability to understand the role of the deputy minister and to communicate that role with charts, quotations and cases made a major contribution to the character of the report. Finally, he and his colleagues have brought a commitment and determination to enlighten the debate on public administration that has been a constant source of enjoyment for me.

I am also very grateful for the assistance of several departments and agencies for lending me staff to do this study. The Department National Defence lent Michael Nelson to the study under the Career Assignment Program. Michael was the Research Director for the study. As the only full-time researcher other than Richard, he played a key role in carrying out the research and drafting the final report. The Office of the Auditor General helped the study by lending John Rutherford on a part-time basis. John undertook some excellent research on the evolution of the accountability system in the federal government and the role of central agencies. In addition, the Office of the Comptroller General lent Reg Heasman on a part-time basis for most of the study. Reg made a major contribution in the analysis and transcription of our interviews with deputy ministers.

Several others made important contributions to the study. Sandy Mac-Laren assembled and organized our computer-based statistical data and carried out a review of accountability literature. Glen Milne advised us on graphics and worked with the Aerographics firm to produce most of the illustrations in this report. Our relentless editor, Kathryn Randle, guided the report to a style which I believe is easily read and understood. Many colleagues in the private and public sectors reviewed our drafts and provided helpful criticism as we formulated our findings and conclusions.

To undertake this kind of research, it is essential to have staff support to arrange interviews and meetings and to help transcribe and edit text. Sharon Crawfold Miller worked with us for the first year to help establish the study, and Danielle Hebert-Roy joined us for the second year and played a vital part in the production of the final report. Finally, I want to thank Cheryl Lojzer of NCMRD for helping me maintain a hectic travel schedule and providing me with vital secretarial assistance.

One of my major aims in doing this study was to create a better understanding of the realities of accountability and management in the federal government. In order to do this, I depended heavily on the goodwill and co-operation of ministers, deputy ministers and advisers to ministers. I have been overwhelmed by the co-operation I have received in undertaking interviews and case studies. Ministers and deputy ministers have a genuine desire to improve the management of the federal government, and I am indebted to them for the frankness and sincerity of their views. Since this information was given to me in confidence, I have made elaborate efforts to ensure that the sources of particular quotations could not be identified, or that the cases we present cannot be linked to a particular minister or deputy minister. Where quotations were particularly sensitive or specific to a minister or deputy minister I have cleared them with the person in question, even though they are unattributed.

Notwithstanding the involvement of ministers and deputy ministers, the contribution of the study team and the advice provided by NCMRD and others, I take full responsibility for the results of this study and the conclusions and recommendations I have provided. I hope that these recommendations will help the federal government to keep deputy ministers accountable.

Finally, I have to note that this research can be regarded as a first step towards a better understanding of the realities of accountability for deputy ministers in modern governments. My hope is that others will have the opportunity and support that I have had to pursue some of these questions, which I have only had time to touch on.

Gordon F. Osbaldeston
London, July, 1988

The Honourable
Gordon F. Osbaldeston
P.C., O.C.

KEEPING
DEPUTY
MINISTERS
ACCOUNTABLE

CHAPTER 1 INTRODUCTION

A ccountability is a familiar concept in Canadian politics. Prime Ministers and their Cabinet colleagues seldom pass a day without pointed reminders from opposition parties, the media, or a host of others that they are accountable for their actions. This is as it should be. Accountability is an essential feature of parliamentary government in Canada. It underpins the operation of our democratic process.

This study deals with one of the critical links in the parliamentary system of government — the accountability of deputy ministers to ministers and the Government. I undertook the study because I am concerned that the accountability system for deputy ministers in the federal government has become confused. Changes have been made to the structure of government and to management of the deputy minister group without due regard to their effect on the accountability of deputy ministers. It has become more difficult for deputy ministers to decide from whom they are to take direction and to whom they must justify their actions. Consequently, it is more difficult for them to support their ministers and to manage departments effectively.

Over the past twenty years, government in Canada has become much more complex than the relatively simple structure that prevailed during the 1950s and early 1960s. The size of the Cabinet has increased significantly with the addition of ministers of state. The Prime Minister's Office has been enlarged and the role of central agencies has changed. New institutions have been added or existing ones expanded to respond to needs such as official languages, access to information or concerns about value for money. More recently, the position of minister's chief of staff was established and parliamentary reforms were introduced.

During this same period, there has been a major increase in the frequency of rotation of deputy ministers among departments. Whereas deputy ministers could once expect to spend more than five years with a department, a tenure of about two years is now common.

1

Many of these changes have been specific responses to the need for better management of public funds, better political advice for ministers, or an increased role for parliamentarians. The changes have enabled the federal government to adapt to new needs and pressures, but they have not been without costs. These costs are evident in the current confusion with respect to the basic roles and responsibilities of Parliament, ministers and deputy ministers.

Parliamentarians are confused about whether it is ministers or their deputy ministers who are accountable to parliamentary committees. Some ministers have established a chain of command that places their chief of staff between them and their deputy minister. Other ministers have been reluctant to publicly accept responsibility for the actions of their officials, even when those actions were within the legitimate bounds of the officials' duties.

There has been a tendency over the past twenty years to downplay the basic principles upon which the parliamentary system of government is founded and to borrow from congressional models of government. Some critics have argued that ministers can no longer be fully accountable for directing large complex departments and that it is necessary that deputy ministers be accountable to Parliament and central agencies for administration. Proposals have been made to make deputy ministers partisan political appointees. The proponents of such changes do not give proper weight to the effect of the changes on key components of the parliamentary system of government, such as ministerial responsibility and the accountability of deputy ministers to ministers.[1]

The purpose of this study is to promote a better understanding of the role and responsibilities of deputy ministers in the parliamentary system of government. To do this, I have pursued three objectives:

——— To map the accountability system of deputy ministers
——— To identify problems in the system
——— If possible, to make recommendations for improvements

The study describes how deputy ministers work within the complex environment of the federal government and how ministers and governments hold them accountable. It covers the fundamental accountability questions that deputy ministers have faced over the past fifteen to twenty years as well as the current problems in their accountability system. I have found some areas in which I am able to make recommendations. However, I would point out that in my view, the most important contribution of this report is its description of the contours in a landscape that is too often viewed in a one-dimensional light.

The less complicated world of twenty years past will not return. The challenge for the federal government and the public service now is to maintain a trusted and competent cadre of deputy ministers who can deal with the necessarily complex realities of modern government. Together, they must take steps to ensure that deputy ministers continue to be accountable and responsive to ministers and have the ability and experience to manage departments effectively.

1.1   RESEARCH APPROACH

Much of the public debate on the subject of accountability over the past ten years has occurred without a complete understanding of the role of deputy ministers and how they work within the accountability system of the federal government. The special feature of this study is that it is based primarily on extensive interviews and case studies with ministers, deputy ministers and others who are serving or have served in federal governments over the past several years. This approach has enabled me to describe the realities of accountability and management in the federal government as experienced by those who work within the system.[2]

The study's research program comprised several projects, including:

Interviews with Ministers, Deputy Ministers and Chief Political Aides

The report draws from more than 120 in-depth interviews, including all current deputy ministers, 28 former deputy ministers, 11 ministers and former ministers, 8 chief political aides, and about 50 assistant deputy ministers and other senior executives from departments and central agencies. The interviewees spanned seven governments over more than two decades.

The interviews are the major source of information for most of the chapters in this report, and a representative sample of quotations from these interviews is presented throughout the report.

Case Studies

The study included 11 case studies dealing with the accountability of deputy ministers. Nine of the cases concerned deputy ministers in the federal government and two involved deputy ministers in the Ontario government.[3] Summaries of most of the case studies are presented in this report. The cases have been disguised by changing the names of departments, programs and other identifiable details.

—— The Accountability System: Institutional Roles and Management
Processes
To profit from the public administration literature, we undertook a
major review of the literature on the federal accountability system
and researched the legal and historical basis for the accountability of
deputy ministers to central agencies. In addition, we interviewed executives of the Privy Council Office, the Treasury Board Secretariat
and the Public Service Commission to understand how they view the
accountability of deputy ministers and to understand how the formal
and informal accountability processes function. The main findings
from this research are presented in Chapter 3.

—— Accountability in the Private Sector: Chief Executive Officers
Many have compared management in the public sector with management in the private sector and have recommended the use of
private sector techniques to improve management in government. To
understand the extent to which there is a basis for such comparisons
and to learn more about the realities of management in the private
sector, we interviewed 21 chief executive officers from a variety of
Canadian companies. The results of these interviews are presented in
Chapters 5 and 6.

—— Parliamentary Reform and the Role of Deputy Ministers
In our initial research on the accountability system it was evident
that parliamentary reform had important implications for the role of
deputy ministers. Consequently, I arranged to have a special study
done on this subject; the study has been published as a separate
background paper.[4]

—— Tenure of Deputy Ministers and Ministers
We undertook a statistical analysis of the tenure of ministers and
deputy ministers. The results of this research are presented in
Chapter 6.

I also gave four speeches that were subsequently published and
distributed to ministers and deputy ministers across the country. The
speeches outlined the research approach and preliminary findings.[5] In
addition, Richard Paton and I made about 20 presentations to various
professional organizations, academic groups, and provincial
governments. The feedback we received from these speeches and
presentations was very useful in formulating my conclusions.

To assist in the analysis of findings, we drew extensively on the
current literature on the role of executives and the dynamics of
organizations. The links between this study and the literature concerning
management and organizations are documented in the end notes. A
complete description of the research methodology used for this study
is contained in a working paper which is available from the National
Centre for Management Research and Development.[6]

1.2 DEFINITIONS: ACCOUNTABILITY, MANAGEMENT RESPONSIBLILITY AND ANSWERABILITY

The difficulty in finding a useful definition of accountability is that in common usage the word may express a range of meanings. Consequently, in our first several interviews, deputy ministers used the word in varying ways. Some deputy ministers said they felt accountable to clients, staff and parliamentary committees. When questioned further on their use of the word accountability, however, they made important distinctions between their obligations to these groups as opposed to their obligations to their minister or the Prime Minister. For example, they did not think that such groups had any authority to instruct them or to assess their performance. Other deputy ministers restricted their use of the word accountability to describing their traditional relationships with the Prime Minister, their minister, Treasury Board and the Public Service Commission.

Further interviews led us to conclude that deputy ministers distinguish among three types of relationships — accountability relationships, management responsibility relationships, and answerability relationships. The consensus among those we interviewed is that these relationships may be defined as follows:

Accountability of Deputy Ministers

Accountability is the obligation of a deputy minister to answer to a person or group for the exercise of responsibilities conferred on him or her by that person or group.

Accountability involves the fundamental question of who is responsible for what and to whom. According to this definition deputy ministers are accountable only to those individuals or groups with whom they have a direct authority relationship based on legislation or convention.

Management Responsibility of Deputy Ministers

Management responsibility is the requirement for deputy ministers to respond to the concerns of individuals or groups within the overall context of their accountability obligations.

Deputy ministers have a sense of responsibility towards clients, staff, provincial governments, other departments, ministers of state, chiefs of staff and other groups.

For example, deputy ministers feel responsible for co-operating with the Commissioner of Official Languages when he is auditing their departments and when they are responding to his recommendations. However, deputy ministers are not accountable to the Commissioner of Official Languages. Their accountability in this instance is to the Treasury Board for personnel management and to their minister for managing the department. Similarly, deputy ministers are responsible for ensuring that their departments are fair, accessible and efficient in dealing with clients. However, deputy ministers are not accountable to clients. They are accountable to their ministers and the government for how they deal with clients.

Answerability of Deputy Ministers to Parliament

Answerability is the obligation of deputy ministers to provide information and explanations to Parliament on behalf of their ministers and the government.

In the parliamentary system of government, deputy ministers are accountable to ministers and ministers are accountable to Parliament. This does not mean that deputy ministers are accountable to Parliament. Deputy ministers have a special requirement to assist ministers to fulfil their obligations to Parliament or parliamentary committees by providing accurate and complete information on department activities and the policies established by the minister. However, it is generally accepted in the parliamentary system that ministers have the right to decide how they will carry out their obligations to Parliament and what role the deputy minister should play to assist them in this regard.

The distinction made by deputy ministers between accountability, responsibility and answerability is critical to maintaining the integrity of the accountability system in parliamentary government. For example, if deputy ministers were subject to instructions or sanctions directly from parliamentary committees they would inevitably be less accountable to ministers and the government. If deputy ministers thought that they were accountable to clients independent of the minister, their actions could undermine the responsibilities of the democratically elected government. The distinction between these three relationships will be maintained throughout this report.

1.3   OVERVIEW: THE ACCOUNTABILITY SYSTEM OF DEPUTY MINISTERS

We use the term "accountability system" to describe the set of accountabilities that deputy ministers must satisfy in carrying out their duties. Clearly, accountability of an individual to more than one person or group contradicts a commonly accepted tenet of good management practice. Yet, this is how the system has evolved. Deputy ministers are faced with multiple accountability relationships.

The accountability system for deputy ministers is illustrated in Figure 1-1. The figure was developed and modified as a result of our interviews, and it was widely accepted by the ministers and deputy ministers we interviewed as an accurate representation of the existing accountability system in the federal government. The chart shows that the centrepiece of the accountability system from the point of view of deputy ministers is their accountability to ministers. Ministers, in turn, have their own accountability relationships. The interdependent roles and relationships involved in this system represent centuries of adaptation of the parliamentary form of government. Figure 1-1 illustrates that deputy ministers are accountable to:

—— the minister because of the provisions of departmental statutes and the Interpretation Act. It is to the minister that the deputy minister owes supreme loyalty;

—— the Prime Minister, who recommends to the Governor in Council the appointment of deputy ministers, and who, with the advice of the Secretary to the Cabinet and the Committee of Senior Officials, assesses the performance of deputy ministers. As the Glassco Royal Commission observed in its report, "the appointment of deputy ministers by the Prime Minister provides a reminder to them of their need for a perspective encompassing the whole range of government ... and emphasizes the collective interest of ministers and the special interest of the Prime Minister in the effectiveness of management in the public service".[7] The Privy Council Office publication "Office of the Deputy Minister" puts it this way, "By convention, however, the Prime Minister has the right to nominate deputy ministers and thereby has the opportunity to discuss their responsibilities with them should he choose to do so. Through the Prime Minister's role in expressing the consensus of Cabinet he may wish to highlight the priorities and objectives of the government and impart his own personal concerns to the deputy;[8]

—— the Public Service Commission, which has the right under the Public Service Employment Act to delegate staffing authority to deputy ministers; and

—— the Treasury Board, which can delegate certain financial and personnel management functions to the deputy minister under the Financial Administration Act, and can require deputy ministers to comply with collective management goals and administrative procedures.

FIGURE 1-1

ACCOUNTABILITY OF THE DEPUTY MINISTER

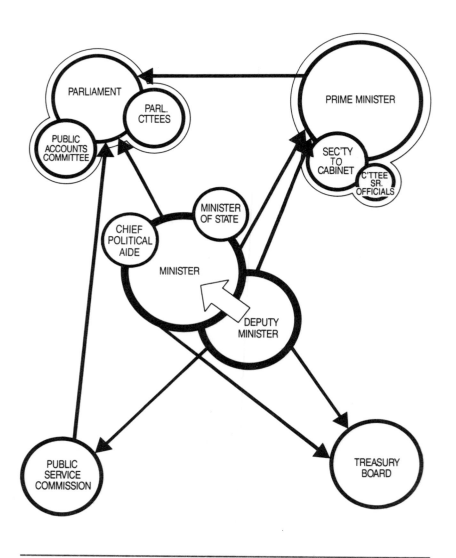

THE REPORT

The accountability system for deputy ministers is the framework for this report. Chapters 2 and 3 provide a starting point for examining the system, by exploring the accountability relationships shown in Figure 1-1 in detail. In describing these relationships I have made a conscious effort to avoid oversimplifying them. They are complex — often to the point of confusion — and I would be doing an injustice to the players and to readers alike if I were to portray them otherwise. The challenge of public administration is provide responsive, effective government in spite of this complexity.

Having described the structure of the accountability system, I turn in Chapters 4 and 5 to an examination of how deputy ministers fulfil their accountability obligations. Conceptually, any accountability process should consist of three stages; the setting of expectations, the pursuit of expected goals, and the holding to account for performance. In the reality of government, the first stage can be incredibly difficult to achieve, casting doubt on how to carry out the second and third. In some cases, the setting of expectations by the minister never happens at all. What implication does this have for the accountability of the deputy minister? How do deputy ministers reconcile this seeming gap in the accountability process with their accountability to the Prime Minister for achievement of overall government goals?

Chapters 4 and 5 examine these questions by describing the role deputy ministers play in helping ministers set and implement their agendas. Chapter 4 identifies agenda-setting as an essential feature of the accountability process and describes the problems that may arise when it does not take place. Chapter 5 focuses on the approaches deputy ministers take in implementing the minister's agenda through the department and explores the challenges they face in carrying out this task.

A recurring theme in this report is the importance of the relationship between ministers and their deputy ministers. In particular, I stress the unique socio-political barriers that must be overcome in order to establish trust as a basis for this relationship. Chapter 6 addresses issues relating to two questions that ministers must ask themselves before trusting their deputy ministers: Is my deputy minister competent? Is he or she going to be loyal to me? In exploring these questions, the chapter covers the final stage in the conceptual accountability process; the holding to account of deputy ministers through assessment of their performance.

These six chapters complete the system mapping and problem identification that were the primary goals of this study. In Chapter 7, I set out the conclusions that I have reached regarding the accountability system of deputy ministers, as well as recommendations that I believe will be helpful in resolving the problems that exist in the system.

2 ACCOUNTABILITY OF DEPUTY MINISTERS TO MINISTERS

T he central relationship in Figure 1-1 is the accountability of the deputy minister to the minister. It is central because everything that the deputy minister does can affect the performance of the minister. Correspondingly, the minister is expected to exercise political control of the department through the deputy minister.

Because this relationship is so important, a large part of this study was devoted to documenting how deputy ministers assist ministers with their responsibilities and how ministers and deputy ministers work together as teams. The aim of this chapter is to describe the nature and dynamics of this pivotal relationship.

The first two sections of the chapter deal with the fundamental responsibilities of ministers and deputy ministers. They provide a context for this chapter and for those that follow. The next section deals with the nature and dynamics of the minister-deputy minister team. The team is at once a tradition-based, hierarchical relationship between a politician and a public servant, and a human relationship. It stands or falls on the ability of two individuals to work within their traditional roles, trust each other and co-operate. The research provided valuable insights into what makes this unique relationship work and why it sometimes does not work.

The final sections deal with some of the current pressures that are making it difficult for ministers and deputy ministers to work together effectively.

2.1 THE ROLE OF THE MINISTER

In the federal government, the power and authority to make decisions with respect to particular departments are provided through statute to individual ministers. These ministers are personally responsible for activities carried out under their authority. Responsibilities include policy development, communication with the public, management of the department, and delivery of programs.

However, ministers do not have absolute discretion in carrying out all of their individual responsibilities. Decisions about their departments that have broad governmental significance must be brought before the Cabinet for approval. The Cabinet is a discussion and decision-making forum of ministers that is led by the Prime Minister. Cabinet decisions are based on the principle of collective responsibility. This principle is rooted in the need for a government to reconcile spending estimates and to stand or fall as a single entity.[1] In practice, this means that the requirements of individual ministers are subject to scrutiny, criticism, or change by other ministers. Although this practice is conventional rather than legal, it is strictly enforced in order to ensure that all ministers will support the issue when it is before the House of Commons. A Cabinet decision is the Prime Minister's view of the consensus of all ministers.

This dual nature — individual and collective — of a minister's responsibilities pervades nearly all ministerial activities and decisions. It is a fundamental determinant of how ministers do their jobs and how deputy ministers assist them.

HOW MINISTERS SEE THEIR ROLE

Ministers assuming their first Cabinet appointment soon find that their responsibilities encompass practically everything in the department. They discover that they do not take charge of a department with a clean slate; instead they assume responsibilities and obligations to clients or the public that may have existed for decades or are prescribed in legislation. When appointed, they have to understand the nature of the public trust that has been given to them and decide quickly how they will carry out the work of the department. Chapter 4 of this report describes this critical first step in the accountability process, which we call agenda setting, in detail.

It is often assumed that because of the many time demands on ministers and the complexity of government departments, ministers do not provide much direction to departments and therefore cannot be accountable for their overall management. Our interviews indicate that ministers rely on deputy ministers to manage departments, but they often provide specific directions on how that management role should be carried out. Ministers use at least five methods to direct their departments:

—— They give general direction on the policy and management priorities of the department. This provides a context within which the department carries out its policy analysis and management functions on behalf of the minister.

—— They respond to problems identified by clients, parliamentarians or other Cabinet ministers by questioning officials and seeking changes in department practices.

—— They provide specific direction to their departments with respect to key priority areas, which could involve developing a new policy; designing a new program; seeking a change to the mandate of the department; making a series of expenditure decisions such as grants or contracts; and improving levels of service to clients.

—— They review and sign Cabinet documents, major submissions to Treasury Board and changes in regulations and approve public announcements and correspondence.

—— They communicate with Parliament, the public, Cabinet and the Prime Minister with respect to all important matters affecting the department.

In practice, ministers do not restrict their interests to policy questions and do not make neat distinctions between policy and management issues. They tend to pay attention to whatever questions are relevant to their priorities, their performance as minister and the fortunes of the Government. They provide guidance to the department on how to carry out a particular portion of the department's mandate, how to be responsive to requests by clients or how to resolve problems identified by the department.

Ministers are regularly involved in management decisions that could affect their relationships with parliamentarians, other Cabinet ministers or clients. For example, they told us of their personal involvement in downsizing decisions, reorganization proposals and changes to programs. This is the day-to-day reality of being a minister in the federal government that is not always visible to the public or to parliamentarians.

Ministers appointed for the first time have a twofold problem. They must not only learn their own jobs but also find out how to work within the structures and processes of government. As one minister noted, "The system is very intimidating to a new parliamentarian or to a minister who doesn't understand it." However, as they gain experience and knowledge of their departments they are better able to determine how and when they should provide direction to the department and when they should rely on the deputy minister to manage on their behalf.[2] In this regard, they said that deputy ministers are responsive to their priorities and try to make sure that the department is sensitive to their priorities and requirements.[3] They can give strong direction to deputy ministers simply by indicating that they don't like something the deputy minister has done. As I once put it in an article:

> "On one occasion I had to give a speech on behalf of my minister. Because I believe strongly that public servants should not be public figures, I tried to avoid being quoted in the press. However, when I opened the newspaper the next morning, there I was, picture and all. Later that morning I had a meeting with my minister. When I entered the room he was reading the newspaper. He didn't look up when I entered. He just kept reading with his head down. I knew something was wrong. Finally, when I sat down he threw the newspaper in the waste basket and said to me, `I didn't realize you were running for office.' I didn't need any more instruction than that to guide me in matters of media relations."

One of the first challenges that ministers face is to balance their responsibilities: as a minister of a department; as a parliamentarian; as a member of Parliament who has to serve and represent a riding; as a party member who has to attend caucus meetings and political functions; and as a member of Cabinet who has to participate in Cabinet meetings and committees.[4] In our interviews with ministers and chief political aides, it was evident that the realities of doing these five jobs within the limits of 24-hour days were both exhilarating and frustrating for ministers.

The challenge for most ministers is to use the deputy minister and department to the greatest extent possible while providing the political direction necessary to ensure that they are responsive to the minister's requirements. Ministers find that they rapidly develop their own political antennas with respect to matters affecting their department. They gather information through their roles as parliamentarians, Cabinet ministers and party politicians as well as their exposure to departmental clients and the media. As one minister stated:

> "My job was to represent the interests of the clients of my department. My real power at the Cabinet table and with the department came from the small communities that my department served. My job was to make sure that the government was responsive to these groups and that the department helped them."

Not suprisingly, ministers feel more confident about providing direction to departments and making decisions once they have become familiar with the business of the department, its programs and clientele. These are typical comments by ministers and chief political aides:

> "There is definitely a danger of being co-opted by the bureaucracy if you don't know what you are doing, but the way you hold deputy ministers to account is easy. You talk to them, you read your briefings, you ask questions, and you make your own decisions."

"Deputy ministers would give their best advice and 80 to 90% of the time the minister would take it. But when the minister wanted to do otherwise, that was the minister's decision."

"We didn't have any trouble with the department. It was our agenda and we just made it clear to the department that these were the minister's policies. There were no problems with the department's responsiveness to these policies. The deputy minister was very co-operative in this respect."

"If there was ever any disagreement between me and the deputy minister, I always won. This was not because of overpowering logic. It was because I was minister."

2.2   THE ROLE OF THE DEPUTY MINISTER

Deputy ministers are the most senior officials in departments. They are appointed to departments by the Governor in Council, on the recommendation of the Prime Minister.

Since the role of deputy ministers is to support their ministers, their responsibilities have the same dual nature as those of ministers. They must support the individual responsibilities of their ministers, but they must also be responsive to the conventions, procedures and regulations that represent the collective views of the Cabinet.

According to the Interpretation Act, a deputy minister or deputy head of a department can undertake any or all of the functions the minister performs, except for such functions as making regulations.[5] This Act, in addition to any specific departmental legislation, establishes the legal basis for deputy ministers to be a key resource for their ministers and the primary link between the minister and the department.

THE DEPUTY MINISTER'S MANAGEMENT ENVIRONMENT

The circles in Figure 2-1 connected to the deputy minister with solid lines are the accountability obligations of deputy ministers as depicted in Figure 1-1. Those with dotted lines represent the various entities to which deputy ministers feel they must be responsive, but to whom they are not accountable. Together, these individuals and groups make up the management environment of deputy ministers. The special case of Parliament and its committees is dealt with later in this chapter.

Deputy ministers are expected by the minister and the Prime Minister to be responsive to the needs and requirements of a variety of individuals and groups. In the interviews, deputy ministers stressed that being responsive to these groups can be very important in the day-to-day management of a department. In some instances the groups become so influential with a minister or the Government that it seems as though deputy ministers are accountable to them. Thus, in government it is

---

FIGURE 2-1

THE DEPUTY MINISTER'S MANAGEMENT ENVIRONMENT

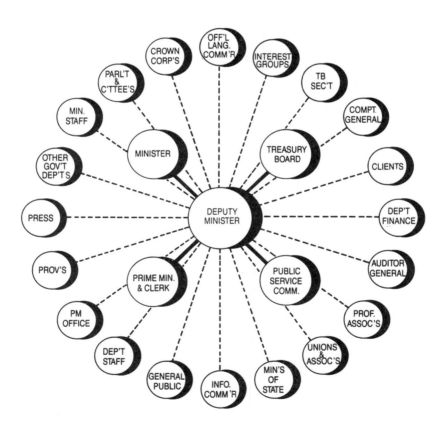

easy to confuse accountability obligations with management responsibilities. One of the challenges facing deputy ministers in this working environment is to maintain these distinctions.

A large part of the job of a deputy minister, be it relative to accountability obligations or management responsibilities, involves negotiating, consulting and communicating with groups that the department depends upon for support or resources. Thus, the capacity of deputy ministers to support ministers depends on their ability to influence groups over which they may have no direct authority.[6] One deputy minister explained the environment in these terms:

> *"In the public sector, the deputy minister has to deal with dozens of groups. It's like an octopus. In one day you can deal with Treasury Board, the Public Service Commission, the Privy Council Office and many others on the same issue. Most of these groups can punish you by withholding something like money or staff. All of these people I have to deal with. These groups hold me accountable to their objectives, but not for achieving my objectives."*

HOW DEPUTY MINISTERS SEE THEIR ROLE

The quotations on the following page illustrate the general consensus among deputy ministers about their role. When speaking of their role, they frequently referred to "The Office of Deputy Minister", a document prepared by the Privy Council Office in 1984. They believe it provides a much needed and accurate description of their responsibilities and accountability relationships.[7] The document defines the three major responsibilities of deputy ministers as policy advice, collective management and internal department management.

Policy Advice The policy advice function usually embraces the development of policy options and recommendations, including the assessment of their political, financial and other impacts. There was widespread agreement among deputy ministers on the general characteristics of this role; deputy ministers are to provide policy options and a thorough analysis of the impact of these options, but it is not their role to perform politically partisan functions such as publicly advocating or defending controversial policy positions. Rather, it is their role to explain the government's policy and thus enlighten the debate. Ministers and chief political aides generally agreed that this is how deputy ministers actually carry out their work.

Deputy ministers feel an obligation to do more than simply advise their ministers; they believe it is their duty to tell ministers what they should hear, whether they like it or not. They feel that they have a responsibility to be aware of major trends or influences that can affect

THE ROLE OF THE DEPUTY MINISTER

POLICY ADVICE

"I am a firm believer in the compelling requirement for the DM to be thorough in laying out options before the minister. Ministers have to make decisions, but the deputy's role is to be exhaustive of the various courses open to the minister. I would go further and say that he must be prepared to express his opinion putting himself in the minister's shoes saying 'this is the option I would propose'."

"The minister is entitled to get a good examination of the issues and recommendations from professional analysts. He is entitled to get information from the deputy about what other people are thinking. He is entitled to recommendations on the best course to follow and why. If the minister, in spite of the advice to the contrary, decides to go another way then that was it. I would not try to undercut him. But I believe it is my duty to give him all the advice I can, whether he wants to hear it or not."

"The DM must listen to the concerns and interests of the minister. He must then use his knowledge of departmental capabilities and policy issues to produce appropriate solutions to bring before the minister. You have to factor that into accountability."

COLLECTIVE MANAGEMENT

"My main job in collective management is to be sensitive to the overall priorities and concerns of the government and to respond to them in my department."

"I think that there are two types of accountability and both are real. There is an accountability to the minister for the minister's agenda and to the broader political agenda, and the accountability to the central agencies for administrative matters is equally real, but different."

"In the last analysis, it is the Prime Minister who holds me accountable. In a more immediate way, it is the minister."

INTERNAL DEPARTMENT MANAGEMENT

"For this department I have a certain accountability to the minister for maintaining this organization's integrity and reputation."

"I have a responsibility for the long-term capability of the department as an institution with a particular mandate or role in the country. I have a responsibility to move ahead of the immediate issues and be ready for the emerging issues or problems which will result from changes such as demographic shifts. A deputy minister could get an 'A' rating in terms of keeping the minister happy and out of trouble and satisfying the central agencies, but you still would not have done what you should have done in maintaining the department's capabilities and developing its staff."

"I pay particular attention to two policy objecives: delivering the public service programs and policy apparatus to the Government, and doing that in such a way that does not compromise the integrity of the public service as a non-partisan professional organization."

the country and ensure that the minister is aware of them. For example, they must be informed of, and ensure that their minister is informed of major demographic shifts, the possibility of rapid increases in energy prices and similar developments with implications for public policy, as well as changes in client needs. Deputy ministers feel they have a professional obligation to outline the options and their implications as completely as possible and to provide ministers with politically sensitive but non-partisan advice. As one deputy minister said:

"My relations with the minister are as good as exist around town. I've only got one aim, to see his ministry humming exactly the way it should. I made a deal with him when I came aboard. I told him, `I am going to tell you the truth. It may not be right, but I will tell you the truth as I see it, and sometimes I won't even be polite. This is the service I can give to you. Whatever you decide to do, unless it is very offensive, I'll do it.' I've told him many times that he is wrong and he has accepted it. The key is he is using me. He is using me to get things done."

Collective Management As stated above, deputy ministers must assist their ministers in carrying out their collective responsibilities with respect to Cabinet. These responsibilities have two components — policy co-ordination and management. The two are discussed separately for the sake of analysis, but they should not be considered as being mutually exclusive. In practice, decisions on one normally require consideration of the other.

The policy co-ordination role of deputy ministers involves activities aimed at ensuring that the department's policies are consistent with broader Government goals and policies. In particular, deputy ministers must ensure that proposals put forward for Cabinet consideration take cognizance of the views of the Prime Minister and other ministers. Typical activities include participation in inter-departmental working groups, attendance with the minister at Cabinet, and consultation or negotiation with other ministers or their officials. Deputy ministers often have to be brokers, reconciling differences between the minister's interests and the concerns of other departments, ministers, central agencies, and the Prime Minister.

The management component of the deputy minister's collective responsibilities has special significance. In supporting the minister's responsibility and authority to manage departmental resources, the deputy minister must also observe government-wide management standards and regulations that have been set by ministers collectively. Further, deputy ministers are given certain financial authorities directly (i.e., not through the minister) by the Financial Administration Act, and they receive delegated authorities for personnel functions from the Treasury Board and the Public Service Commission.

Deputy ministers agreed with the description of their formal accountability links to the Prime Minister, Treasury Board, and the Public Service Commission as set out in Figure 1-1. They regard these obligations as part of the requirement to achieve particular government priorities, maintain overall standards of management, and ensure the degree of consensus and cohesion necessary for the Government to function. The accountability of deputy ministers to the Prime Minister, to Treasury Board and to the Public Service Commission is discussed in detail in Chapter 3.

Internal Department Management   The third responsibility of deputy ministers is to manage the resources of the department under the general direction of the minister.

Deputy ministers feel that their primary role in department management is to ensure that the department responds to ministerial priorities and that the administration of the department is carried out in a way that reflects the minister's direction and interests. To ensure that management questions are dealt with in a manner consistent with the minister's priorities, deputy ministers are careful to have the minister review any question that could be considered politically sensitive. In addition, if a department has become overly institutionalized or unresponsive, deputy ministers have an important role in ensuring that the department begins to respond positively and quickly to the minister's direction. One deputy minister explained her accountability to the minister for department management this way:

"I told the minister, 'We'll keep you squeaky clean in terms of the Financial Administration Act and the departmental statute and we will tell you whenever we think that things are not fitting within the bounds. We will give you our best advice from a public servant's point of view. But, we freely admit that ministers can see more dimensions than we can. When you decide, we will work to the beat of your drum.'"

It was evident from the interviews that the strong public service ethic of serving and supporting the minister has not diminished over the years. This ethic also provides an important safeguard that enables ministers to rely on deputy ministers and officials to refer to them questions that require political judgement. As one deputy minister put it:

"I insist that activities of the department which could be of concern to the minister, the subject of public reaction or questions in the House are submitted to the minister for approval."

Deputy ministers said that part of their responsibility is to inform the minister when particular actions would endanger the proper discharge of certain functions of the department or its ability to carry out its mandate. Many of them said that as deputy head of a department they had a responsibility to the Prime Minister and the Government to ensure that the department functioned effectively and that it had the continuing capacity to serve future ministers.

The role of deputy ministers in providing a responsive and effective department for the minister is discussed in detail in Chapter 5.

A COMPLEX ACCOUNTABILITY SYSTEM

The foregoing discussion of the role of deputy ministers begins our exploration of the fundamental dilemma of their accountability system. In the event of a conflict among any of the four parties that may call the deputy minister to account, which one will be given primacy?

The implications of this dilemma can be unsettling for ministers and their deputy ministers. Can the minister rely on the deputy minister if accountability to one of the other players may at some point take precedence? There was widespread agreement among deputy ministers that, in practice, accountability to their ministers was the most important, unless that accountability was specifically over-ridden by the Prime Minister (see Chapter 3). Nonetheless, the fact of multiple accountability remains as a potential irritant for ministers and deputy ministers as they work at creating a good relationship.

2.3   THE MINISTER-DEPUTY MINISTER TEAM

In this section we begin our examination of the role and nature of the minister-deputy minister team. This theme carries on to the next section, which deals with the inherent difficulties of bridging the gap between politicians and officials.

In reading these sections it is useful to keep a few facts in mind. First is the complex accountability system of the deputy minister. The minister-deputy minister team must be forged in the context of this sometimes conflicting system. Second is the working environment of the deputy minister as depicted in Figure 2-1. The amount of time available for team-building is severely limited by the demands on the minister's and deputy minister's schedules. Further, the constant scrutiny and judgement by media, parliamentarians and others strain the human element of the relationship. Finally, the research shows that the life of a minister-deputy team is seldom longer than two years. During the period 1984-1987 it averaged less than one year. Thus, the relationship must work effectively almost immediately if the team is to accomplish anything during its brief tenure.

THE ROLE OF THE MINISTER-DEPUTY MINISTER TEAM

In Canadian government, a good decision requires an analytical element, a political, non-partisan element, and a partisan political element. For a given policy or program proposal, a department prepares an assessment of the options, the costs, the implications for existing policies or other priorities of the Government. There is also an analysis of the impact on client groups, the provinces and so on. This departmental non-partisan political advice should be based on the deputy minister's knowledge of the priorities of the minister and the Government and a strong understanding of the social and political realities facing the department.

The minister and chief political aide bring both a non-partisan and a partisan political perspective to decisions. This includes an assessment of the political priorities of the Prime Minister and the Government, the implications for the minister's personal agenda, the views of caucus and constituents, and the relationship of the policy or program to the electoral fortunes of the minister.

The role of the minister-deputy minister team is to bring all these elements to bear on departmental policy, program, and management decisions. If an effective working relationship is not present, the quality of these decisions will suffer.

Both ministers and deputy ministers made it clear that there is no substitute for a strong working relationship between ministers and deputy ministers for achieving responsive and effective government. Directions from the Prime Minister, scrutiny by Parliament, guidelines from the Treasury Board or sophisticated management systems cannot make up for poor communications, mistrust or ineffective teamwork between a minister and a deputy minister.

Almost all those interviewed agreed that when ministers and deputy ministers are able to work well together, the accountability system functions very well. However, when a minister and deputy minister are not able to work well together, both face difficulties carrying out their responsibilities.

Ministers who do not seek and obtain the necessary advice from their departments are vulnerable to criticism by Parliament, the public and other ministers because they may lack essential information. Deputy ministers who are not able to develop a co-operative working relationship with their minister have difficulty managing the department or balancing their minister's interests and the requirements of central agencies. Without this teamwork, it is very difficult to maintain the proper balance between ministerial direction of the department and the collective management requirements of government. One experienced deputy minister summed it up:

> "There is some sort of mythology out there that ministers come in and say, `Here is the policy', and everybody goes marching off to that tune. In actual fact, it is a highly interactive process. That is when you find that the minister and deputy minister make a powerful team. When they don't have that they get into trouble. They have to understand each other and respect each other but not necessarily like each other. When you have all that, you have a powerful synergistic relationship."

One of the most revealing findings from the interviews was the degree of consistency between ministers and deputy ministers when they spoke about the importance of the minister-deputy minister working relationship. This was as true of the ministers and deputy ministers who served in the 1960s and 1970s as it was of those who served in the 1980s. The importance of the relationship as a foundation for the deputy minister's accountability to the minister has not changed significantly over the past 30 years.

HOW MINISTERS AND DEPUTY MINISTERS VIEW THEIR RELATIONSHIP

The only analogy used by ministers and deputy ministers to describe their relationship was a marriage. They chose this analogy because it implies an intimate partnership where each has particular responsibilities and both parties are highly dependent on each other. Ministers and deputy ministers said that unlike a marriage they did not have to like each other, but they did have to have mutual respect, be able to work together, and trust each other.

A deputy minister who had worked with many ministers put it this way: "The minister-deputy minister relationship is like a marriage. You have to work at it every day."

A minister who has had several portfolios said: "The minister-deputy minister relationship is more demanding and more all-encompassing than a marriage. You are dependent on each other for practically everything that goes on in the department, and to a large extent your career depends on this relationship."

Another deputy minister, who was relatively new to the public service, tried to compare the minister-deputy minister relationship with other situations in which he had been involved:

> *"Perhaps I am overstating it, but the minister-DM relationship is more like a marriage. I have never seen a relationship apart from a marriage that is so fundamental to society. There is a fundamental difference between the intensity and importance of this relationship compared to the role of senior executives in other organizations."*

During the course of a career, most deputy ministers work with a variety of ministers with different personalities, interests, working styles and views of the public service. One of the most interesting and challenging parts of the work of a deputy minister is to adapt and adjust to variations between ministers. The working styles of ministers vary widely. Some prefer oral briefings while others prefer to read detailed documents. Some want their briefings in French and others in English. Some like to have long discussions about the department. Others prefer short, issue-focused meetings. One deputy minister who had worked for about a dozen ministers described how he adapted to these differences:

> *"A lot depends on the personality of the minister. I've never worked the same with any two ministers. You have to know the personality of the person you are dealing with. You have to adapt the process you are using to the personality of the minister. What is most important is that at the end of the exercise there is a common knowledge, as best we can establish it, of where we are going."*

To a considerable degree, deputy ministers judge their success in relation to their minister's performance. As one deputy minister put it, "I'm the minister's deputy. If he is in trouble, I'm in trouble." Deputy ministers do not associate themselves with a particular policy approach or option. Rather, they view their achievements in terms of helping a minister achieve a policy or program direction that he or she has chosen. They take considerable pride and satisfaction from the fact that they are able to work with a variety of ministers and serve them well. One deputy who had a very good working relationship with a minister noted, "My relationship with one minister was so good that we could speak for 30 seconds and communicate an entire idea."

2.4   MAKING THE TEAM WORK: THE IMPORTANCE OF TRUST

Within a few hours or days of their appointment, ministers meet their deputy ministers and receive their first briefing on the department and their responsibilities. Given the demands on them, ministers have only limited time to direct the department. They quickly find that they must use the deputy minister's expertise and knowledge if they are to meet their responsibilities. One minister described his initial exposure to his role:

> "I looked around at who could help me fulfil these onerous responsibilities as a minister. I found that backbenchers were too expensive. Any help they give you will cost you in a grant or a new facility. Your Cabinet colleagues are too busy; they have their own constituencies and ambitions. Your political staff can only perform limited functions, mostly of a partisan or quasi-partisan nature. Funds for hiring political advisers are limited, therefore you can only afford these advisers on an exceptional basis. I was left, like it or not, with the deputy minister. He knew the department and how to work within the government."

Ministers face a dilemma in entrusting their departments to deputy ministers. Ministers have been charged with significant and often unfamiliar responsibilities, yet they know that they have little hope of discharging them entirely on their own. They must work with a deputy minister who in all likelihood has very little personal or professional background in common with them. In the case of a new government, ministers may have to work with a deputy minister who has assisted an outgoing government to develop and implement their policies. If they give their trust to a deputy minister who serves them poorly, their careers could be damaged. But if they willfully ignore vital advice that turns out to have been right, their current portfolio could be their last.

The difficulty of quickly establishing a relationship based on trust under these circumstances should not be underestimated. It is clearly a different circumstance than that experienced by say, a board of directors when hiring a new Chief Executive Officer, particularly when one considers that the performance of a minister is often judged in the House of Commons on a daily basis, rather than a quarterly or annual basis. Ministers know that the consequences of their decision to trust a deputy minister may be in newspaper headlines the next day.

It is not surprising, therefore, that ministers sometimes have difficulty trusting their deputy ministers. Some ministers overcome these initial suspicions, some do not. Notwithstanding the challenges of establishing trust between a minister and deputy minister, it is clear from our interviews that it is vital to do so. Without trust, it is almost impossible to establish a good working relationship. One deputy minister summed it up this way:

> *"I've had about 24 ministers and I can't generalize. They were all different. The need for a high level of trust, however, is paramount."*

A chief political aide had a similar view:

> *"I don't think there is a generic answer to the question of accountability of deputy ministers to ministers or what works well. It all depends on people, situations and events. Every situation is different, and people have to be able to adapt to each situation and work out the necessary relationships. However, one could say that the relationships between ministers and deputy ministers work best when there is a good deal of personal security and self-confidence among the various key players. The chief political aide has to be secure in his mind about his relationship with the minister. The minister has to be secure in his rapport with the Prime Minister. And there has to be trust between the minister and the deputy minister. When you have all that the system works pretty well."*

Deputy ministers, too, face a dilemma if the minister does not trust them, because they cannot exercise control of their departments and manage effectively unless they have the confidence of their ministers. A minister who does not trust the deputy minister will find other avenues through which to implement his or her agenda. A lack of confidence may be expressed by extensive filtering of the deputy minister's advice by political assistants or by dealing directly with departmental staff without the deputy minister's knowledge, but in either event the deputy minister is effectively neutralized.

The case study entitled "Earning the Minister's Confidence" illustrates how one deputy minister overcame the initial reluctance of the minister to work with him. The actions of the deputy minister in this case are typical. Experienced deputy ministers recognize that tacit acceptance of their competence and good intentions constitutes a leap of faith for ministers. They try very hard to demonstrate that they are both willing and able to support the minister.

DIFFERENT APPROACHES TO THE TRUST QUESTION

In our interviews with ministers and deputy ministers we found three distinct attitudes among ministers with respect to the degree of trust they placed in their deputy minister and the officials in the department.[8] These differences had important implications for their working relationships and for achievement of ministerial goals.

Ministers who assume deputy ministers are loyal and supportive professionals who will respond to political direction The predominant view among ministers is that deputy ministers are loyal, non-partisan professionals and vital to the success of the minister. They start with the assumption that their deputy minister is competent and will be sensitive and responsive to their direction. In these cases ministers devote the first few months of their tenure to establishing a good working relationship with the deputy minister, clarifying their role and that of the deputy minister and chief political aide, and then providing the overall direction for the department. Not surprisingly, these ministers were generally the most experienced and most successful ministers.

Two typical quotations illustrate the views of these ministers.

"I believe that public servants are loyal to their ministers and will respond to the direction of ministers. I would be very suspicious of a deputy who tried to be my ideological bedfellow. I want professionals working for me who will provide me with the kind of advice they would provide any minister. Part of that professionalism is the political sensitivity to understand the situation that the minister is faced with and the kind of advice he or she needs."

"As a minister you basically have two choices. You can work with the department or work against it. If you try to work against it you are doomed to failure. If you work with it, you have at least a chance of success. My philosophy is to work with the department and get it working for me. If you look around you will find that this is what successful ministers do."

The result of this approach was well illustrated by one deputy who quickly developed a good relationship with the minister.

"My relationship with my minister was cemented overnight. I was very lucky. A deputy of this department is only as useful as his influence with the minister allows him to be. The minister understood the nature of our relationship from day one. That meant that I could get on to priority two. Some deputies never get there.

EARNING THE MINISTER'S CONFIDENCE

A Deputy Minister (DM) was appointed to a large Department that was administratively complex, highly decentralized, and difficult to manage. The DM had no experience or knowledge of the issues facing the Department, nor did he have a network of personal or professional contacts in the Department or in the community and client groups it served.

The Minister had been in place for a few years. He was experienced, energetic, and well briefed. During his time with the Department he had become acquainted with dozens of people both at headquarters and in the field, and he did not hesitate to call them himself. A previous DM had had considerable difficulty adapting to the Minister's style and was replaced.

The new DM's first and most immediate agenda item was to earn the Minister's confidence while at the same time learning about the Department. It was clear to the DM that unless this was accomplished, his ability to assist the Minister and to provide leadership and direction to the Department would be severely inhibited.

THE DM'S APPROACH

The first task the DM set for himself was to learn about the policies, programs and clientele of the Department. It was clear to him that given the

Minister's encyclopedic knowledge of the Department, he could never gain the Minister's confidence unless he knew more about these areas. This task involved long hours during his first year in office. In addition, he travelled extensively and met with a large number of representatives from client groups.

The DM made a point of being very responsive to any ministerial requests. He placed a lot of emphasis on reliably meeting his commitments to the Minister and supporting the Minister's initiatives. In his briefings to the Minister he used the frank, no-nonsense style that the Minister preferred. This approach appealed to the Minister, and he gradually began to share confidences with the DM. The DM also used his knowledge of central agencies and of other ministers (he had worked closely with six ministers in previous posts) to assist the Minister to implement his agenda. This was one area where the Minister particularly valued the DM's expertise.

A crucial challenge for the DM was to make effective use of his assistant deputy ministers (ADM). The Minister's practice of dealing directly with departmental officials had over the years created a "DM-bypass" that could be used by ADMs whenever convenient. This direct route to the Minister, combined with the ADMs' strong connections with the community of technical experts in the country and, in some cases, their good relations with influential Members of Parliament, created a formidable challenge to the DM's formal authority. The arrangement also made it difficult for the DM to hold his staff accountable and to manage them on behalf of the Minister.

As his knowledge of the Department increased, the DM began to take decisive steps to exert management leadership. He provided clear direction on specific issues within the Department and asserted himself forcefully with his ADMs. He made his expectations apparent and followed up when matters were not proceeding to his satisfaction. When he was unhappy with a particular issue, he did not hesitate to send a strong memorandum to the responsible party. He also instituted a system of quarterly reporting against plans to facilitate holding his subordinates to account, and he dedicated time to reviewing these detailed documents.

At the end of his first six months in the Department, the DM judged that although much work remained to be done, he had come a long way towards winning the confidence of the Minister. The Minister knew that the DM would give him the information that he wanted on any issue. In terms of policy advice, even though the Minister might not agree with the DM, he knew that he could trust him. Having established a more secure base for exercising his authority, the DM was now better able to support the Minister with his policy agenda and to pursue administrative improvements within the Department.

OBSERVATIONS

The experience of this DM highlights the importance of earning the Minister's confidence for managing a Department. While the new DM was nominally in charge of the Department, he was unable to exert his influence on any matters of consequence until he was considered trustworthy and competent by the very experienced and knowledgeable Minister, and until he had established himself in a clear management leadership role.

The case also illustrates the mutual dependence inherent in the Minister/DM relationship. Despite his initial reluctance to rely upon the DM in departmental matters, the Minister recognized that he needed the DM for frank policy advice; to move his policies and programs through the central agencies; and to negotiate with other departments and their ministers.

You have to have the minister's confidence. He assumed competence and that we could work together. This is something that we haven't lost, to my knowledge."

Ministers who are initially suspicious of deputy ministers and the department but change their views This group is much smaller than the first. Some ministers start with suspicions about the power of deputy ministers or their loyalties. These concerns are more prevalent after a change of government and are often held by ministers who have had little experience with government. One minister noted that he started with this view because, as an opposition member of a parliamentary committee, he observed the close relationship between a particular minister and deputy minister. He interpreted this to mean that the deputy was politically partisan. Only later did he learn that his deputy minister would serve him in the same loyal manner as he had served the previous minister.

These ministers may try initially to use their political staff to control the department or to lead major policy initiatives. However, after working with a deputy minister for a period of time, many change their minds. As their deputy ministers demonstrate loyalty and commitment to the government in power, the ministers realize that their initial preconceptions were not accurate. In some cases they come to trust their deputy minister but still remain suspicious of deputy ministers as a group.

One minister described how irritated he had been in his first few weeks as minister when a deputy minister insisted that he include a certain paragraph in a speech. The deputy minister argued that if the minister did not include the paragraph, it could create trouble for him with clients and possibly even the Prime Minister. After thinking about it the minister realized that the deputy minister was going to considerable lengths to protect his interests, not trying to undermine him. Another minister who changed his views over his first year put it this way:

"A lot of ministers came in with strong preconceived notions, mainly negative, about the public service. Unfortunately, some do not change their views. But, I don't think that I could find a `political' deputy that would have the managerial skills and knowledge of government that I need as minister to do my job. I learned about the DMs and their value to ministers by watching and observing how other ministers used their DMs and which ones were successful."

Ministers who start out mistrusting their deputy minister and remain uncomfortable working with the deputy minister and the department Some ministers start with suspicions about the reliability and competence of the public service and deputy ministers and do not change their views. The minister's experience as a member of Parliament may have shaped his views about the political loyalties and power of deputy ministers. These concerns may be reinforced by initial difficulties or misunderstandings between the minister and deputy minister or by a personality clash. If a deputy minister is unresponsive or insensitive, an already difficult situation may be aggravated.

If a deputy minister does not have the experience or department knowledge necessary to support the minister and is forced to fall back on his general knowledge of government or the specific knowledge of assistant deputy ministers, it is more difficult to establish a good working relationship with the minister.

Mistrust by a minister of a deputy minister creates a particular pattern. The minister tries to rely on political staff to manage the department; the staff in turn reflect or reinforce their minister's suspicions. Such ministers do not delegate to the deputy minister. They do not seek the advice of the deputy minister, particularly with respect to policy. They are extremely suspicious when the deputy minister points to concerns that central agencies or the Prime Minister may have, and suspect disloyalty or collusion. The minister and the minister's office try to manage the decision-making process in areas such as contracting, staffing and grants. Finally, ministers who mistrust their deputies and the public service tend not to discuss priorities or their agenda for the department with the deputy minister. The results were described by one deputy minister:

"When I arrived, the department was still traumatized from the difficult relations that had existed with the previous minister and his office. The former deputy had managed to insulate most of the department from the worst of these problems but it was not possible to prevent the relationship from affecting the overall morale in the department. The new minister and my predecessor had solved many of the problems by the time I arrived, but there was still a lingering effect to be dealt with."

As several ministers noted, it is unfortunate that some ministers have to pass through this learning period before they can make full use of the public service. The fact is that the most successful ministers learn how to use their deputy ministers and are certainly not controlled by them.

Ministers said that ministers who do not learn how to direct and use their officials face significant difficulties trying to work with Cabinet, Parliament and the press. Their approach to managing the department creates real risks for themselves and for the Government. On the other hand, deputy ministers without the experience, knowledge or sensitivity to assist a hostile minister are of limited value to the minister or the Government. Those who find themselves in this situation are usually moved, but a poor working relationship with their minister has a negative effect on their career and that of their minister.

THE POLICY ADVICE CASE

The new Deputy Minister (DM) of a large department had no prior knowledge of the Department or its field of operations. He had been DM of two other departments but this position was by far the most complex.

THE DEPARTMENT: SPECIALIZED POLICY EXPERTISE

The Department administered a significant portion of the federal budget. A high proportion of this budget was in the form of non-discretionary, statutory and inter-governmental obligations. The clientele included a wide cross section of the Canadian population.

The work of the Department involved a wide range of highly specialized technical areas. The areas were staffed at the operational and management levels by professional and technical experts who had extensive training and expertise in their fields. Structurally, the Department was composed of several branches that were relatively autonomous management organizations in their own right. Previous DMs had often found it difficult to keep current with activities in the branches.

THE ROLE OF THE DEPUTY MINISTER

The DM felt that he faced three major challenges in carrying out his role.

First, he had to provide policy advice and support that was relevant to the Minister's interests. Second, he had to learn enough about the Department and its activities to provide appropriate and effective direction and guidance to his officials. Lastly, he had to find a way to harness the Department's policy development capability without allowing his lack of technical knowledge to hinder the policy process.

THE POLICY ADVICE ROLE

The DM saw his two principal roles as being a resource manager and a policy adviser. Since the Department did not face any major management problems, his strategy for departmental management was to make sure that good people and good systems, including frequent reporting and good internal audit, were in place. With this responsibility controlled to his satisfaction, he was able to concentrate his attention on the policy advice function, which was of primary concern to the Minister. The DM worked for two ministers during his tenure and was involved in several national policy issues.

Given the technically diverse range of policy issues and the professionally knowledgeable senior officials in his branches, the DM decided that he could add the greatest value to the policy development process by acting as a facilitator rather than as a filter. Based on broad policy guidance from the DM (who had done his best to determine what the Minister wanted to accomplish), assistant deputy ministers and directors general contributed suggestions for the departmental policy agenda. The DM would then chair meetings where he saw to it that debate on the priority that should be assigned to the various issues was conducted in a reasonable way. The results of these meetings were presented to the Minister for his consideration.

Although the DM reserved the final recommendations to the Minister for himself, he rarely overruled the advice of his professional staff regarding the facts of a technical issue. In these instances, he added non-technical advice, based on his extensive policy background and his knowledge of the Minister's priorities and concerns, to the advice emanating from his branches. Rather than trying to master the intricacies of technical issues himself, he used departmental experts to state the details of their case directly to the Minister. His role was to decide which officials would be involved and at what stage an issue should be presented.

Despite the often highly technical issues that were brought to the DM for the Minister's consideration, he nonetheless felt completely accountable to the Minister for any recommendation that he made. He felt that it would be up to him to find a way, when he put forward a recommendation or signed a document, of satisfying himself that he could defend it.

OBSERVATIONS

The major challenge for the DM was to ensure that policy proposals emanating from the professionally-oriented branches were sensitive to the current or anticipated wishes of ministers.

For the DM, the policy advice function included four specific roles. As anticipator, he managed the policy development process so as to provide support for issues that he thought the Minister would be interested in pursuing. As articulator he added non-technical advice to proposals emanating from within the Department. As adviser, he provided counsel to the Minister on anything in which the Minister was interested. As implementer, he directed departmental action on policy choices made by the Minister.

This approach to policy advice enabled the DM to provide the Minister with technically sound and politically sensitive policy advice and to assist ministers to achieve their major priorities.

MANAGING THE POLICY PROCESS

The new Deputy Minister (DM) of a Department was a career public servant. She had been an assistant deputy minister and an associate deputy minister in various government departments and had spent several years as a senior executive in central agencies.

THE DEPARTMENT'S POLICY ENVIRONMENT

The Department had a large budget and provided thousands of grants to various groups. The programs of the Department were the object of considerable political interest at the riding, provincial, regional and national levels. The Department had a particularly strong relationship with its clients. Because funding decisions were often heavily influenced by coalitions of political interests, they required the minister's political judgement in order to determine which groups or areas would receive government support.

In keeping with the nature and mandate of the Department, the DM saw her primary responsibilities as managing the policy process as opposed to providing expert policy advice.

THE DM'S ROLE IN THE POLICY PROCESS

It was clear to the DM that she was accountable to her Minister for the provision of policy advice. Soon after her appointment, however, she realized that the mandate of the Department and the nature of its work raised particular challenges for her policy advice role.

Because the Department was large and complex and dealt with many different programs and policy issues, the DM could not possibly keep current on the facts and implications of each issue. Further, political considerations not known to the DM, such as trade-offs between Cabinet ministers, were often the deciding factor in an issue. In this context, the DM decided that she should be responsible for managing the policy process to ensure that the Minister was presented with a complete set of facts, options and implications for each issue, whether the issue originated inside the Department or not.

The DM was not, therefore, the proponent of any particular policy choice to the Minister. Rather, she managed the formulation of policy options. She listened with the Minister to the facts and arguments presented by her officials, and assisted the Minister with non-partisan advice in weighing those options and in choosing a course of action. Similarly, when officials presented an issue to the Cabinet, it was generally an ADM who played the lead departmental role. The DM was normally present, but in the role of supporter.

While she did not feel accountable for decisions made by ministers, the DM viewed herself as fully accountable to the Minister for ensuring that the appropriate information and advice was provided for ministerial decisions, including the views of the Department, other ministers, and interest groups.

During her tenure, the DM worked for two ministers who had considerable differences in background and views. Both ministers, however, were comfortable with the policy management style practised by the DM, largely because the ministers could feel confident that they were being given a full view of all available perspectives on an issue. They were able to judge for themselves the political sensitivities of options for various constituencies and were able to take account of departmental analyses and recommendations as well.

OBSERVATIONS

The DM found that she could best carry out her responsibilities for policy advice by managing the policy process.

By leaving front-line policy development and advocacy to her senior officials, the DM was able to maintain the flexibility to work with the minister to find policy options that best met the needs of ministers, clients and the Department; attend to her general management responsibilities within the department; and contribute to other issues of interest to the government.

THE VEHICLE SAFETY CASE

An experienced Deputy Minister (DM) was appointed to a new Department in the midst of a vehicle safety controversy. Consumer groups were pressing the Minister to use his authority under department legislation to introduce safety improvements to automobiles that would save the lives of an estimated 25 children annually. Unions protested that jobs would be lost when companies passed the associated cost increase on to consumers. While public safety was clearly the Minister's and the DM's first concern, the issue had to be managed carefully, since a furor over job losses could prevent a timely resolution of the problem.

THE INTEREST GROUPS

The structure of interests in the politics and economics of vehicle safety consisted of manufacturers, major parts suppliers, unions and broad-based lobbies, such as a consumers' association. All were well organized and informed on the facts of the child safety issue, although each had a different set of statistics to support their arguments. Each could mount an effective media campaign.

In 1985, a consumers' association passed a resolution calling for specific child-oriented safety improvements on new vehicles. A working group, consisting of representatives from the major interest groups as well as government officials, was formed to study the problem. Despite divisions of opinion, the working group was able to make some broad recommendations to the Minister. The principal recommendation, which was accepted by the Minister, was that the Department form a committee to study the technical and economic aspects of the issue.

THE ROLES OF THE MINISTER AND DEPUTY MINISTER

In early 1986, additional pressure to resolve the issue emerged when the Minister promised a House of Commons committee that revised regulations would be in place by the end of the year. Subsequently, developments occurred that made that promise very difficult to fulfil. While the advisory committee had reached consensus on general principles, a serious split had emerged regarding implementation. Public interest groups supported quick action. The industry, supported by the unions, was con-cerned about the implications of revised regulations for jobs. The Minister and his newly appointed DM were soon visited by senior labour representatives who expressed strong fears of major job losses if new regulations were imposed. Thousands of jobs were at risk, most of which were in the Minister's home province. Nevertheless, the Minister's resolve to act in the interest of public safety remained strong, and his instinct was to act quickly.

The DM understood his responsibility to the Minister as one of simultaneously implementing the new regulations and managing the controversy. He knew that hasty action could trigger one side or the other to go public in a way that would greatly increase the uncontrollability of the issue. The DM did not participate as a regular member of the advisory group. He preferred to leave that work to his departmental experts, but he was briefed regularly on the results of the group's deliberations. The DM made personal interventions at strategic points in the negotiation process so as to manage the controversy.

After initial discussions between the Minister and the DM, the Minister was quite satisfied to leave the management of the issue to the DM, and to provide support when required. The Minister also had other major preoccupations that could not easily be delegated. The Minister's agenda was fully occupied with the need to advance the cause of several difficult pieces of legislation, some of which had a tortuous history. In addition, the

Minister had been assigned special responsibility by the Prime Minister to manage the difficult politics of implementing an inter-provincial highway construction agreement.

By mid-1986, the positions of the major players had hardened considerably. The union/industry coalition maintained its threat of job losses. They believed that an information campaign to encourage more diligent use of seat belts could reduce injuries to the same extent as installation of new safety devices. They called for more time to study the issue. The public interest groups strongly opposed any further extension of time. If there were further delays they would go to the media.

WILD CARDS: UNRELATED EVENTS SHAPE THE ISSUE

The Minister's and DM's position in favour of public safety was strengthened considerably by the emergence that summer of a political disaster that befell one of the Minister's colleagues. That Minister had made a serious misjudgement, allowing a potential safety hazard to continue rather than risk financial damage to an industry. Media coverage had made both the Government and the industry look bad. It was clear to the Minister (and to the interest groups) that he had to come down quickly and firmly on the side of any public safety issue. The DM was able to use the increased public awareness and concern about public safety issues to force a con-

sensus among the advisory group participants. This enabled the Department to introduce safety measures while dealing with employment adjustment problems.

RESOLUTION OF THE ISSUE

A regulation was announced that called for a graduated installation program for the safety devices. This allowed industry to make adjustments with a minimal loss of jobs. The Department compensated for the delayed installation period by providing funds for a public information campaign designed to increase public awareness of child safety in vehicles.

OBSERVATIONS

In this case, the DM played a major role in negotiating a change in a regulation affecting child safety in vehicles. However, in managing these negotiations he was clearly working on behalf of the Minister and had a very clear understanding of the Minister's priorities and preferences.

The Minister in this case did not have the time to deal personally with the safety issue, but he made his views on the priority of public safety over job security clear to the DM. This clear statement and understanding of goals between the Minister and DM permitted the Deputy Minister to manage the issue, knowing that he was accountable for resolving it within the Minister's stated guidelines.

THE MINISTER-DEPUTY MINISTER TEAM: THREE CASES

The three cases described in the accompanying boxes illustrate how three deputy ministers used different approaches to provide advice to their ministers. In these three cases they were successful in adapting to the circumstances of the department and the minister's requirements. To support their ministers effectively, deputy ministers must be able to recognize the unique requirements of different departments and ministers. They have to be able to adapt to the particular priorities of each minister and to come to some agreement with them on the role that the deputy minister, the minister's staff and other department officials should play.

PRESSURES ON THE TEAM

In the final sections of this chapter we move outside the minister-deputy minister team to study three groups that ministers and deputy ministers say have significant potential to influence their effectiveness. Chief political aides, ministers of state, and Parliament (in particular, parliamentary committees) can strain the relationship between ministers and deputy ministers by engaging in activities that are beyond their legitimate roles. In doing so, they may interfere with the accountability of deputy ministers to their ministers.

2.5   CHIEF POLITICAL AIDES: POLITICAL AND PARTISAN SUPPORT

An important determinant of the relationship between ministers and deputy ministers is the role played by the minister's political staff. The provision of competent political staff to ministers can increase the partisan advice and support available to them, thereby reducing pressure on the deputy minister or department to provide partisan political advice.[9]

Our interviews with chief political aides included chiefs of staff from the current government and executive assistants or senior policy advisers to ministers in previous governments. We found that the basic questions that deputy ministers face in dealing with political advisers are similar from government to government.

We asked ministers how they used their chief political aides and what distinctions they made between the role of their political staff and that of the deputy minister. We asked political aides how they viewed their role in relation to the minister and deputy minister. Finally, we analysed how the introduction of the chief of staff concept by the Government in 1984 affected the accountability relationship between ministers and deputy ministers.

MINISTERS' VIEWS

Ministers believe that their chief political aides are vital to their role as ministers. The work of chief political aides reduces pressures on ministers. They provide partisan political advice that deputy ministers cannot appropriately give. Several ministers commented that they insisted that their chief political aide work co-operatively with the department and that the department co-operate with the chief of staff.

Ministers often take the initiative to ensure that the relationship between political staff and the department works well from the start. Meetings to establish ground rules and working relationships among the major players are common. Two ministers explained how they did this:

"In one department I gave clear instructions to my political staff that if they lorded over the public servants in the department, they would be out. At the same time I made it clear to the senior executives in the department that my staff should be treated as an extension of me in my political role as minister. I explained that the chief political aide should be the alter ego of the minister. The workload in the department is so large that it is necessary for my staff to work with the department just to keep the work moving. I have to rely on their discretion and that of the deputy to decide what has to come to me for review or approval. After some initial difficulties, my political staff are working well with the department and I am able to play the role of manager of the process."

"The minister cannot manage everything and relies on political staff to alert him to errors and to achieve particular priorities. You must insist that they understand your priorities and your views on key issues. There should be a healthy tension between the political staff and the department, but it should be a very open relationship."

DEPUTY MINISTERS' VIEWS

Most deputy ministers agreed that ministers need competent partisan political advice and support. The experience of deputy ministers with chief political aides was mixed. Some found that political aides had complicated their accountability linkages with the minister without adding much ministerial support. Others found that political staff were an asset to them, the minister and the department.

Bad Experiences Several deputy ministers expressed serious concerns about the role of chief political aides, believing that they had jeopardized their working relationship with their minister. When the minister and chief political aide did not trust the public service or the deputy minister, the minister's office tended to become an intermediary between the minister and the deputy minister.

Deputy ministers noted that some chief political aides had little knowledge of government or expertise in policy. They did not have the skills to carry out their role. This, combined with the tendency of some chief political aides to try to run the department, caused difficulties. One deputy minister put it this way:

"I never met with the minister alone without the chief political aide present. On one occasion a key document that I forwarded to the minister was intercepted by the chief political aide and not even seen by the minister. The minister's staff went directly to my staff for information. I have gone to meetings where the minister's staff and my staff had documents I had not yet seen. How could I carry out my accountability obligations to my minister when there was someone operating between me and my minister? Who is accountable when they were receiving orders directly from the minister's office? This was a very unhealthy accountability structure and the worst part about it was that it made the minister very vulnerable.

"I had problems reminding the chief political aide that there is a Public Service Employment Act. I had to talk to the minister and inform him that my job was to keep him out of trouble and that there was a piece of legislation that exists on staffing. My minister tended to trust and depend on the chief political aide as opposed to the deputy minister and the department. He was suspicious of the bureaucracy."

Some current and retired assistant deputy ministers were very disturbed by the role ministers' staff sometimes play in department management. Staff from the minister's office, for example, may call people at junior and middle levels to obtain advice and information. If senior officials are not aware that such contacts are taking place, these back channels may enable middle level staff to influence the minister's office directly and achieve their own agenda without challenge from senior management. In addition, in areas such as grants or contracts the minister's staff may try to direct officials without consulting the deputy minister or the minister. This can create real problems for the reporting relationships between the deputy minister, assistant deputy ministers and the minister.

Good Experiences The majority of deputy ministers found that a strong minister's office and a knowledgeable and competent chief political aide could be useful. Several deputy ministers said they could take issues to the chief political aide and get a political reading without having to take the minister's time. The minister's staff could assist the minister and the department to steer complex issues though the political process. In these instances the chief political aide helped ministers accomplish their priorities and did not adversely affect the accountability of the deputy minister to the minister.

Deputy ministers have to work at building a good relationship between the minister's office and the department. They must develop good operating principles such as circulating key documents to the minister's staff and encouraging open communication between department staff and the minister's office. We found instances, for example, where the minister's staff and the department had established operating principles that enabled the minister's aides to discuss issues directly with departmental officials. Where this degree of co-operation was established, ministers and deputy ministers were satisfied with the level of teamwork that resulted. Three quotations from deputy ministers are typical of the views of about 70 per cent of the deputy ministers we interviewed:

> *"I talked with the minister about the chief political aide not becoming a screening device. I said I could not support the minister adequately if the chief political aide was a go-between. I explained that if I needed him I would pick up the phone and call him. He said he would do the same. I have had a very good working relationship both with the minister and chief political aide."*

> *"I had a solid working relationship with the chief political aide. He is excellent. He raised serious political considerations and I tempered my advice by paying attention to them, but he didn't discount the policy substance and management side of it."*

> *"I am of the school of thought that if the minister gets good political advice from his staff, I can do my job better. If he doesn't, then there is a void and the minister may want me to do more of that job than I may want to. In this respect I was luckier than most of my colleagues."*

VIEWS OF THE CHIEF POLITICAL AIDES

The eight current and former chief political aides we interviewed had considerable political and government experience and were generally regarded by ministers and deputy ministers as successful at their jobs. They believed that their role was to serve the minister and that their credibility and influence lasted only as long as they were seen as being able to assist the minister. Most of these aides indicated that they did not see themselves as intermediaries between the minister and the department. Instead, they saw their role as providing the kind of partisan advice that the department could not provide. In most cases these chief political aides established good working relationships with the department, enabling them to assume some of the minister's burden without interfering with the accountability of the deputy minister to the minister. All the chief political aides emphasized the importance of teamwork between the minister, deputy minister and the minister's staff.

> *"I was not there to overrule the department's advice. They had a responsibility to present their views to the minister. I did not always agree with them, but I would never try to force the department to go through me to the minister. The minister was his own man and I would never say I was speaking for him. But the department could use me to get a good sense of how the minister would feel about an issue, and they did."*

> *"The minister has 10,000 people who will tell him what's good for the department, but no one to tell him what's good to get him re-elected. That's my role."*

> *"It works really well when the minister, chief political aide and deputy minister have their own networks and they are working on a common agenda. This has to be reinforced with regular meetings to determine where the department is with respect to particular agenda items."*

> *"The majority of chief political aide situations in my view don't work. This is largely because of the inexperience of the minister's staff."*

Most of the chief political aides noted that the most successful aides had worked previously with their ministers, knew the policy area or department and had some knowledge of the federal government. There was some concern expressed about the difficulty of recruiting and keeping quality staff because of the intense demands of the job and the tendency of some ministers to select people who may not have the skills necessary for the job.

THE CHIEF OF STAFF CONCEPT

In 1984, the Progressive Conservative Government revised the chief political aide concept when they established the position of minister's chief of staff. The reason for this revision was to provide better partisan political advice to ministers and better management assistance in terms of running the minister's office. The concept of chief of staff was to a large extent a formalization of what some ministers in previous governments had done through special contracts. Under the new system, ministers and ministers of state can hire chiefs of staff and pay them at a level equivalent to the salary of an assistant deputy minister. The enhanced status of these political advisers and their availability to all ministers have created new opportunities and problems for the accountability relationship of deputy ministers to ministers.

The experience with the chief of staff concept has been instructive. We estimate that about one-third of chief political aides have developed good working relationships with the deputy minister and the department. In another 30 to 40 per cent of cases the chief of staff has performed a role equivalent to that previously performed by an executive assistant at a lower rate of pay. Finally, in the remaining 30 per cent of the cases, the chief of staff has created substantial problems and significantly damaged the working relationship between the minister and deputy minister.

Most ministers, deputy ministers and chiefs of staff said that the chief of staff is more likely to provide support to the minister when the following conditions are met:

—— The minister ensures that the roles of the political staff and deputy minister are mutually understood and promotes co-operation between the political staff and the department.

—— The chief of staff has a good rapport with the minister and is able to provide partisan advice and support that reflect the minister's interests and requirements.

—— The chief of staff is experienced in the policy area or has a good knowledge of government and the political process and how to work with the deputy minister and the department.

—— The deputy minister establishes an approach to dealing with the minister's staff that enables good communication between the minister's office and the department within the confines of the accepted reporting relationship between the deputy minister and the minister.

In summary, the chief of staff role has increased the potential for ministers to obtain good partisan political advice and support. Problems can emerge, however, when ministers select chiefs of staff without the experience, expertise and attitude required for this difficult job and when the conditions are not in place to make it work.

2.6   MINISTERS OF STATE: ADDED COMPLEXITY

A second potential source of strain on the minister-deputy minister relationship is the presence of ministers of state. In 1970, the Ministries and Ministers of State Act provided a legal basis for two kinds of ministers of state: ministers of state who head a ministry of state (e.g. Minister of State for Science and Technology) and ministers of state to assist (e.g. Minister of State for Agriculture).[10] The remarks in this section are primarily about the latter.

Since 1970, the number of ministers of state has grown continually. As of July 1988, there were 16 minister of state assignments. These were filled by 13 ministers of state, some of whom covered off two assignments. Ministers of state are often appointed to give higher profile and Cabinet representation to special interest groups. They are also seen as a means to enhance political control over an increasingly complex public service. However, they have added a new complication to the role of deputy ministers and their to their working relationsips with ministers.

In strict legal terms, only the minister is accountable for a department and the deputy minister is accountable only to the minister. Although their legal status is quite different from that of department ministers, ministers of state do sit in Cabinet and are permitted to have a chief of staff. Thus, the hierarchy is not as clearly established in Canada as it is in Britain, where junior ministers do not sit in Cabinet, and their careers are heavily influenced by the senior ministers to whom they are responsible.

Our interviews with ministers, deputy ministers and chief political aides indicate that ministers of state add a level of complexity to the traditional accountability relationship between a deputy minister and a minister. Ministers of state raise new and difficult challenges because of the ambiguity surrounding their role, conflicts between them and their ministers, and confusion with respect to the accountability of deputy ministers to ministers of state. Deputy ministers and chief political aides find that the addition of ministers of state can create problems in terms of policy co-ordination and allocation of responsibility.

THE DEPUTY MINISTER AS BROKER

Deputy ministers are increasingly expected to perform the role of broker between the minister and the minister of state, by helping ministers manage their relations with ministers of state. They find this role time-consuming and difficult. One deputy minister estimated that he spent about 50 per cent of his time carrying out this role. Another spent eight to ten hours each week to advise ministers of state on matters related to proposed expenditures or policy initiatives and to ensure he maintained their co-operation and good will.

The following quotations illustrate the difficulties experienced with respect to ministers of state:

> "The issue of multiple ministers is a problem. The senior minister has overall accountability. Junior ministers always have a need for a larger piece of the pie than they are usually given and they want autonomy and they want to be perceived as being autonomous. This really makes for complicated relationships. I had to keep peace in that family and that was an important part of my role."

> "It is inhuman to deal with more than one minister. Each has his own ego. You not only have to give them equal time and attention, you must also ensure that one does not feel less important than any of the others. Then you have the potential clash of their individual desires and you find yourself in the middle of it all like ham in a sandwich. I've had a senior minister wanting to go one way and another minister wanting to go in another direction and I'd be in the middle. It would be so much easier if I had only one minister."

> "The number of linkages in a portfolio with two or three ministers makes a very complex arrangement. Each minister has a chief of staff. The making of connections is an important part of the job. My job was to interpret where other people were coming from. I'd persuade them to get together and talk it over. I was frequently saying that they should set up something for them to get together."

> "I don't really know what to do with ministers of state. But, I do know that in many cases they do not reduce the work of the ministers. There are major personality differences that can cause considerable problems for the department and the minister's staff."

DILEMMAS WITH RESPECT TO MINISTERS OF STATE

Deputy ministers pointed out that while their primary accountability is to the minister, some felt a sense of accountability to ministers of state. Certainly, ministers of state expect deputy ministers to respond to their requirements. This confusion was not the major concern of deputy ministers; they were more concerned about the time required to support ministers of state and to co-ordinate among ministers. It adversely affected their ability to serve the minister and to manage the department. They saw ministers of state as another factor that could undermine their attempts to build a strong working relationship with the minister. Some deputy ministers were concerned about the recent trend in appointing associate deputy ministers to work for ministers of state. In legal terms, the associate deputy minister is still accountable through the deputy minister to the minister of the department. In practical terms ministers of state will likely regard associate deputy ministers as their deputy ministers.

Ministers of state are often frustrated by a role that leaves them in no-man's land somewhere between a parliamentary secretary and a minister. Many have no specific area of authority and have difficulty gaining access to the expertise of the department. It is not surprising that many ministers of state do not willingly accept their junior minister status. Instead they strive to carve out an area of autonomous decision-making authority and push for an associate deputy minister or senior assistant deputy minister to assist them in their responsibilities.

Despite these concerns, the ministers we interviewed did not expect to see any change. In fact, they recognized that there was political advantage in appointing ministers of state. They thought governments would continue to appoint them to provide Cabinet representation for various groups and regions. On a more positive note, one minister said that he had gained considerable experience as the minister of state in a department before being appointed minister of that same department.

The success of a minister of state appointment depends on a number of conditions: whether the senior minister actively directs the minister of state, who in turn is willing to accept the direction and authority of the minister; whether the personalities of the individuals are compatible; whether the minister of state has some expertise to contribute; whether the minister and minister of state have similar policy views; and, finally, whether a clear role or area of authority can be defined for the minister of state with appropriate departmental support. Without these conditions, ministers of state do not reduce the burden on ministers; rather, they create difficulties.

2.7   THE DEPUTY MINISTER'S ANSWERABILITY TO PARLIAMENT

In 1986 several parliamentary reforms were introduced following publication of the Report of the Special Committee on the Reform of the House of Commons (McGrath Report). These changes resulted in the third source of new challenges for the working relationship between ministers and deputy ministers. Through a change in the standing orders, House of Commons committees are now permitted to initiate their own enquiries and to issue reports on the results. In addition, the Government must now respond formally to the recommendations of these committees when requested to do so by the committee. As a result of these parliamentary reforms, the level of committee activity has increased dramatically over the past two years, and the demands on ministers and deputy ministers to justify or explain department policies have increased substantially.

Ministers and deputy ministers recognize that deputy ministers have a strong obligation to provide accurate and complete information to parliamentary committees and to help ministers to explain departmental policies and programs. However, they distinguish between the accountability relationship of a deputy minister to a minister and the requirement for deputy ministers to provide information to parliamentary committees.

To investigate the impact of parliamentary reform on the role of deputy ministers, I arranged for a special study to be carried out.[11] The implications of parliamentary reforms for the accountability system are described in detail in that report. The findings of the special study are consistent with the results presented here, which are based on our interviews.

THE PUBLIC ACCOUNTS COMMITTEE

Deputy ministers generally distinguish between their answerability to the Public Accounts Committee and their answerability to other parliamentary committees. Because of the traditions surrounding the Public Accounts Committee, they believe it is largely their responsibility to explain department management activities on behalf of the minister and to respond to criticisms of department administrative practices. However, deputy ministers noted that in many cases ministers have significant influence on management practices and decisions with respect to contracts, grants or programs. The requirement that deputy ministers support their ministers precluded them from identifying who was responsible for particular decisions. Thus, they thought it was impractical and undesirable to separate the deputy minister's responsibility for administration and management from the minister's responsibility to direct the department. Consequently, deputy ministers believe they attend Public Accounts Committee meetings on behalf of their minister and the Government and not in their own right.

IMPLICATIONS OF PARLIAMENTARY REFORM

Our interviews with ministers and deputy ministers revealed four findings with respect to the answerability of deputy ministers to parliamentary committees under the reformed system.

—   Ministers and deputy ministers are more conscious of the requirement to provide information to parliamentary committees than they were prior to the reforms. Because ministers often do not have time to attend committee meetings, deputy ministers devote considerable time to preparing for committee meetings and briefing committees, thereby assisting ministers to discharge their obligations to Parliament.

—   Most ministers and deputy ministers do not believe that parliamentary reform has substantially changed the primary accountability obligation of the deputy minister to the minister.

—   Deputy ministers and ministers are concerned about the confusion created by parliamentary reform with respect to the role of the deputy minister in the parliamentary system. This is largely because some parliamentarians and ministers do not understand the role of deputy ministers in supporting ministers in the discharge of their parliamentary obligations.

—   An active and demanding parliamentary committee can create strains in the working relationship between ministers and deputy ministers when ministers do not carry out their responsibilities to parliamentary committees; when ministers and deputy ministers have not agreed on the role and obligations of the deputy minister with respect to the parliamentary committee; or when there are strong efforts by committee members to make deputy ministers accountable to them or to attack the minister through the deputy minister and department officials.

Deputy ministers accept the obligation to provide information to parliamentary committees. Some stated that they were delighted to be able to work with knowledgeable committee members who show an active interest in the department. However, ministers and deputy ministers are genuinely concerned about the growing confusion with respect to the role of deputy ministers in the parliamentary system. One chief political aide conveyed his minister's views:

"There is a fundamental difference between the way the minister sees the authority of the committee and the way the committee sees it. The committee believes they can call whomever they want to testify. The minister believes that he is responsible for the department and can send anyone he likes to represent him. This is a difference in views that has to be settled at the highest levels."

Despite some conflicts between ministers and parliamentary committees and some confusion with respect to the accountability system, it is important to note that we found many cases of healthy and spirited rapport between committees and departments and instances where committees perform a valuable function in identifying issues and providing a vehicle for various groups to express their views. We also found that when ministers establish clearly that they are responsible for a department and define the role of the deputy minister with respect to the parliamentary committee, they can establish a good working relationship even if they are dealing with a hostile committee.

To sum up, the challenges facing deputy ministers in fulfilling their obligation to answer to Parliament have increased substantially over the past few years. To assist ministers with their accountability to Parliament, deputy ministers must carefully balance the requirement to provide complete and accurate information to parliamentary committees with the requirement to serve and advise the minister and/or the Government in confidence. If ministers and deputy ministers do not reach an understanding about their roles and obligations with respect to Parliament, they will inevitably run into problems with parliamentary committees.

2.8 FINDINGS: ACCOUNTABILITY OF DEPUTY MINISTERS TO MINISTERS

The ministers we interviewed did not report having any difficulty holding deputy ministers accountable to them. In fact, ministers seldom thought in terms of accountability when referring to their deputy ministers. Instead, they tended to think in terms of whether they had a good working relationship with the deputy minister, whether the deputy minister and department were responsive to their priorities, and whether the deputy minister helped the minister carry out his or her responsibilities.

The accountability of deputy ministers to ministers is critical to democratic and effective government. Yet many of the changes to the structure of government that have been introduced in the past twenty years have increased the difficulties faced by ministers and deputy ministers in working together as a team. The complexity of the government environment and the multiple accountabilities and responsibilities of deputy ministers can create strains in the relationship between ministers and deputy ministers.

If chief political aides become intermediaries between ministers and their deputy ministers, it is difficult for the deputy minister to ensure that ministers receive their advice undistorted by ministerial aides. When deputy ministers are requested to support and respond to ministers of state who are in conflict with their minister, complications emerge with respect to the accountability of the deputy minister to the minister.

Both ministers and deputy ministers said that the likelihood of their being able to perform their roles successfully increases substantially as their knowledge and experience in a department grow. However, they added that the high rate of turnover among ministers and deputy ministers made the aquisition of such knowledge and experience extremely difficult.

In summary, deputy ministers are better able to respond to ministerial priorities and assist them to manage departments effectively when there is a good minister-deputy minister working relationship. We found that a good working relationship depends on the following elements:

———   There is a shared understanding of the role of the minister and deputy minister that is continually reinforced by specific actions.

———   Both the minister and deputy minister have some knowledge and experience of the department and are able to establish a common agenda and implement it.

———   There is a considerable degree of trust, co-operation and open communication between the minister and deputy minister as well as the chief of staff and minister of state.

———   The deputy minister is capable of providing the necessary policy advice and management support for the minister to achieve his or her priorities.

When these conditions are in place, ministers and deputy ministers have no accountability problems. Ministers direct departments. Deputy ministers provide advice and support to their ministers and manage the department on behalf of the minister. Ministers seldom think about keeping their deputy minister accountable. Instead, they focus on how to achieve their priorities or agenda with the deputy minister's support.

CHAPTER **3** ACCOUNTABILITY
OF THE DEPUTY
MINISTER TO THE
PRIME MINISTER
AND CENTRAL
AGENCIES

I n this chapter we conclude our examination of Figure 1-1 by looking at the
accountability of deputy ministers to the Prime Minister, the Public
Service Commission and the Treasury Board. These three relationships
are central to the deputy minister's collective management responsibility.

Chapter 2 introduced the concept of collective management
responsibility by explaining that in parliamentary government, ministers
must work within the context of Cabinet policy to achieve their priorities.[1]
Departmental policies must be consistent with overall Government
policies and must be co-ordinated where necessary with the policies of
other departments. Also, ministers must ensure that their departments
implement programs within the constraints of government-wide
management goals and standards. This latter requirement includes a
host of obligations, ranging from financial management and contracting
standards to affirmative action and bilingualism goals. Deputy ministers
are accountable to the Prime Minister and to their ministers for helping
them to achieve their collective management goals, which include
matters of policy and administration.

Two themes underlie this chapter. The first is the continuing
requirement for deputy ministers to reconcile their collective
management obligations with the needs of their departments and the
goals of their ministers. The combination of strong personalities, diverse
goals, and multiple accountabilities is certain to produce conflict from
time to time. Because each conflicting party is able legitimately to claim
the deputy minister's accountability, deputy ministers must rely on
experience, knowledge and judgement to resolve disputes.

The second theme follows from the first: there are limitations to
using formal, documented controls as a means of securing the
responsiveness and accountability of deputy ministers. Regulations
and standards are essential in the federal government. They can enhance

the effectiveness of departmental operations and help retain the confidence of the public and Parliament in the probity of departmental activities. However, at the level of the deputy minister, the complexity and ambiguity of demands often makes rules less reliable than judgement for resolving conflicts among competing forces. By requiring deputy ministers to comply with rules and regulations to solve complex problems, governments may diminish the quality of solutions. Deputy ministers become accountable for following rules rather than for finding the best solution using their own judgement.

We begin our exploration of these themes with a brief review of how ministers and deputy ministers normally share the work in carrying out their collective management responsibilities. The remainder of the chapter is devoted to the accountability of the deputy minister for collective management.

3.1 MINISTER AND DEPUTY MINISTER: DIVISION OF COLLECTIVE MANAGEMENT RESPONSIBILITIES

Ministers are responsible for the overall management of a department and the accomplishment of its major legislative functions. However, the division of duties, authorities and responsibilities between ministers and deputy ministers with respect to collective management obligations is complicated. In some areas, deputy ministers alone have authority delegated from the Public Service Commission or Treasury Board, whereas in other areas ministers have full authority. For example, the Public Service Commission limits the involvement of ministers in the staffing process by delegating staffing authority to deputy ministers but not to ministers. Similarly, the Financial Administration Act provides for the assignment of personnel management functions and the delegation of some financial administration responsibilities to deputy ministers alone.[2] Ministers have full authority for other aspects of department management, such as the submission of Cabinet documents or proposals to Treasury Board and signing off the main estimates of a department. The authority of deputy ministers in these areas is limited by the Interpretation Act.

Most of the ministers we interviewed recognized the importance of their departments working within established government policies and central management processes. However, it was clear that ministers regarded their primary responsibility as carrying out the department's functions and serving its clients. From the perspective of ministers, complex and detailed central agency controls or co-ordination requirements can interfere with the discharge of their primary departmental responsibilities. Ministers saw their role as bringing the perspective and needs of farmers, fishermen, Indians or consumers to Cabinet and ensuring that the department and the Government were responsive to these clients.

Ministers rely on the collective management abilities of their deputy ministers. They expect the deputy minister to ensure that the department is responsive to clients, to obtain the support of central agencies when necessary, and to help them stickhandle policy, program, or funding proposals through Treasury Board or the Cabinet system. One former minister described how his deputy minister used his network to speed resolution of bureaucratic tangles:

> *"I have little patience for paper and I did not have the time to barter with bureaucrats. My deputy minister knew the system and could use his contacts to get around some of the problems with central agencies. He could also use his contacts to advise me when a personal intervention on my part was required."*

Ministers are often in a hurry. Pressure from various groups and questions from Parliament call for immediate and often specific responses. The institutional structure established to manage collective issues does not always facilitate rapid reaction. This means that deputy ministers must continually balance collective management requirements with the minister's urgencies.

In brief, ministers normally count on deputy ministers to satisfy collective management requirements and to ensure that those requirements do not prevent the department from responding to ministerial needs. The fact that these two conditions may sometimes be mutually exclusive should be borne in mind while reading the next three sections of this chapter.

3.2   THE DEPUTY MINISTER'S ACCOUNTABILITY TO THE PRIME MINISTER

Almost all the deputy ministers we interviewed believed they were accountable to the Prime Minister. This accountability flows from their ministers' collective responsibilities to the Government as a whole.

> *"In theory, the accountability of the deputy minister is clearly to the current Government and to the Prime Minister as the representative of that Government. I think in practice this is not so clear. I feel accountable to my minister on a daily*

basis to a degree that the theory does not take adequate account of. That doesn't create problems as long as the minister and Prime Minister are together and on the same track. But I would say that I am accountable to the Prime Minister in the last resort."

"There is definitely an accountability line from the deputy minister to the Prime Minister. It is difficult to navigate, but it is there. If you do not report to the Prime Minister himself, you must keep the Privy Council Office informed, so that they can inform the Prime Minister."

There is no question that when the Prime Minister sets out explicit goals for the government they are followed by deputy ministers. Equally, there is no doubt that the Prime Minister can only concern himself in a specific way with key and/or critical matters that involve the collectivity of ministers.

HOW DO DEPUTY MINISTERS FIND OUT WHAT THE PRIME MINISTER EXPECTS OF THEM?

Despite the important role that deputy ministers play in achieving overall government priorities, we found that few deputy ministers received specific direction or priorities with respect to their departments upon appointment. Of the 55 deputy ministers we interviewed, fewer than half a dozen received clear directions from the Prime Minister or Clerk of the Privy Council as to objectives for their department. The cases where deputy ministers were given a clear mandate or set of priorities involved departments facing a crisis or where the Prime Minister and Cabinet wanted a major policy or organizational change.

Most deputy ministers said they had been appointed without much warning and simply arrived at the department after not much more than a brief conversation with the Clerk of the Privy Council. After that they were on their own. In recent years deputy ministers have had the opportunity to prepare a statement of their priorities and forward them to the Privy Council Office (PCO). In most cases deputy ministers discuss this statement with their minister.

Although most deputy ministers felt a strong need for better guidance from the Prime Minister or the Clerk of the Privy Council, they recognized that this is very difficult. To a large extent their priorities and approach to the department have to be shaped by their particular minister and the specific situation of the department. Consequently, it is very difficult for the Prime Minister or PCO to tell them what their priorities should be, except in unusual cases. As one deputy minister said:

"One of the problems of providing priorities to deputy ministers from the centre is that there has always been a concern whether the PCO has the capacity to be knowledgeable about the environment of a particular department that would allow them to focus on the right priorities and objectives. It is an enormous management problem and challenge for the centre to be able to focus on this heterogeneous array of government programs across so many departments."

Most deputy ministers recognize that they have to develop their own priorities and approaches to managing a department, basing them on the minister's agenda; the specific problems facing the department; the various concerns expressed by central agencies and other organizations; signals provided by public announcements, events, budget statements or speeches from the throne about the Government's priorities; information provided by the Clerk of the Privy Council on priorities of the Prime Minister and the Government; and when available, the mandate letter from the Prime Minister to the minister.

THE ROLE OF THE CLERK OF THE PRIVY COUNCIL AND SECRETARY TO THE CABINET

The Clerk of the Privy Council and Secretary to the Cabinet is the most senior official in the federal public service. The position is normally filled by a person with a broad range of experience at senior levels in departments and central agencies. The individual is appointed by the Governor in Council on the advice of the Prime Minister.

The Clerk of the Privy Council carries out three major functions in the federal government: Secretary to the Cabinet; deputy minister to the Prime Minister (i.e., deputy head of the Privy Council Office); and head of the public service. The person is therefore a key adviser to the Prime Minister.

He or she is responsible for providing a secretariat function to Cabinet and Cabinet committees; assisting the Prime Minister and Cabinet to co-ordinate policies for the government as a whole; and providing advice and support to the Prime Minister for key functions such as machinery of government, security, and senior appointments. In this last function, the Clerk of the Privy Council is advised on performance appraisal, assignments and salaries for deputy ministers by the Committee of Senior Officials (see Chapter 6). The Clerk of the Privy Council has important responsibilities in providing a role model for deputy ministers and public servants, establishing standards of behaviour for the public service, and ensuring that minister-deputy minister teams are working satisfactorily.

Deputy ministers believe that the role of the Clerk of the Privy Council is to assist the Prime Minister to communicate the overall priorities of the Government and to hold deputy ministers accountable for meeting the expectations of the Prime Minister and the Government. They see the role of the Clerk of the Privy Council as a critical link between their ministers and departments and the collective interests of the Government and the Prime Minister. Deputy ministers noted the importance of the regular weekly meetings between deputy ministers and the Clerk of the Privy Council for this purpose. As one deputy minister said:

> *"The Clerk of the Privy Council is the key person for determining the overall performance, traditions and co-operation between deputy ministers. I feel tremendous responsibility to him, but not as a direct player."*

THE PCO AND THE PRIME MINISTER'S OFFICE: AN ESSENTIAL SEPARATION

Over the past 20 years a clear distinction has developed between the role of the Privy Council Office and that of the Prime Minister's Office (PMO). The tradition is that the Clerk of the Privy Council and the staff of the PCO are professional public servants. By virtue of their non-partisan nature, they are able to serve any Prime Minister. The PCO is the Prime Minister's principal link with the public service.

The PMO, on the other hand, provides partisan political support and advice, and its officials are usually changed by an incoming Prime Minister. The PMO is not normally the vehicle used by the Prime Minister to give operational direction to deputy ministers.

Deputy ministers said that when there is a conflict or confusion of roles between the PCO and the PMO, it is more difficult to carry out their responsibilities effectively. They expect the Clerk of the Privy Council to instruct them on behalf of the Prime Minister. When players in the PMO take on this role as well, it is difficult for deputy ministers to know who speaks with authority about the Prime Minister's priorities.

One deputy minister who dealt with PCO and PMO on a regular basis explained the dilemma:

> *"I took the traditional line that my job is to work through the PCO to the Prime Minister. The PMO were apparently unaware of any such procedure between a deputy and PCO. The PMO would phone me directly and ask for things. They would attend meetings, then call me up afterwards and say let us know what is going to happen. I, being a traditionalist, would phone the PCO and say `I've been asked by PMO for a briefing note.' I would send it to the Clerk of the Privy*

Council and have him deliver it. From the PMO point of view I was not very co-operative. But, that was the position I took. It was a judgement call of whether you should maintain the traditional system or change it. I feel that there is a legitimate partisan role and a legitimate non-partisan role which are very distinct. That is my own understanding of government. But, I suspect the policies and procedures in these matters are changing in a way which may be a permanent change."

Another deputy minister, who had a crisis in his department that caused problems for the Government, found that when a number of different players get involved in an issue, roles and expectations become unclear. He said:

"A lot of accountability is through middlemen. You have very gentlemanly sessions, but at the end of it you are still very uncomfortable because accountability is so diffused. A lot of the accountability (i.e., to the minister, Prime Minister, Treasury Board) is through middlemen. There are things you just cannot see and many undercurrents."

DEALING DIRECTLY WITH THE PRIME MINISTER

On occasion, the Prime Minister assumes responsibility for an issue that would normally fall within a minister's mandate. In such cases the deputy minister's accountability for that particular issue is directly to the Prime Minister. For example, a Prime Minister may decide to intervene personally in a particular aspect of federal-provincial relations. When that happens, departmental officials find themselves working directly for the Prime Minister. The departmental minister may or may not be involved in the issue.

There were major differences among departments in the frequency which they dealt directly with the Prime Minister. Deputy ministers of smaller or medium-sized administrative departments found that they dealt with few issues that involved the Prime Minister. One such deputy said:

"I've never seen the Prime Minister alone in eight years as a deputy minister."

Another deputy minister said:

"My view is that the Prime Minister looks to me to manage this area and not cause him any trouble."

In departments dealing with major government priorities or key policy questions, deputy ministers often felt accountable on a day-to-day basis to the Prime Minister. For example, two deputy ministers who were working on priorities that were important to the Prime Minister said:

"The feedback is fairly direct when working on a high profile issue of concern to the Prime Minister. It appears in the paper the next morning and you know whether you have been successful and how the Prime Minister will react."

"I was involved in meetings with the Prime Minister and the minister more frequently than most deputy ministers. I don't know how often, but probably once every two or three weeks. The whole structure of accountability to the Prime Minister was very clear. There was a link back to the Privy Council Office almost every other week on some issue. We met with officials of the Privy Council Office and the Prime Minister's Office frequently because our item was on the agenda of the First Ministers' Conference."

THE MINISTER OR THE PRIME MINISTER? ACCOUNTABILITY CONFLICTS

Most deputy ministers did not have much difficulty balancing their accountability to the minister and the Prime Minister. However, a few deputy ministers faced major problems resolving situations involving conflict between the two. In one case the deputy minister disagreed strongly with a particular policy proposal of the minister because he thought it would hurt the Government. The deputy minister felt that the Prime Minister had the right to know that there was considerable disagreement between himself and the minister on the question. He said:

"The Prime Minister should have an indication of what kind of advice his minister is proceeding on. The Prime Minister is certainly entitled to that information. The question is, how does he get it? Should he rely exclusively on the Privy Council Office, or is there some permissible rapport between the Prime Minister's Office and the deputy minister?"

In another case a deputy minister believed that a particular administrative action by a minister would cause the Government a great deal of embarrassment. After agonizing over this, the deputy minister concluded that:

"In a situation of a potential conflict between a minister and the Prime Minister, the deputy minister is bound to the Prime Minister."

A third case involved a deputy minister's collective responsibility for policy co-ordination. Deputy ministers must consult and inform other deputy ministers about proposals that could affect their departments' activities. The norm of co-operation is strongly instilled in deputy ministers and is important if the Cabinet is to function effectively. On occasion deputy ministers are faced with conflict between these obligations and the instructions of a minister:

"I have lived in my bones the tension between my loyalty to my minister and the loyalty for collective management. For example, in order for the minister to implement parts of his political strategy, the minister did not want me to consult with other departments or central agencies."

There have been several situations in the past 15 years where strong deputy ministers were appointed by the Prime Minister specifically to keep a new or inexperienced minister out of trouble. In such instances the deputy ministers clearly felt they were more accountable to the Prime Minister than to the minister. One deputy minister described such a situation this way:

"In two cases over more than a decade as deputy minister I went to the Prime Minister about my minister. Both cases concerned the activities and conduct of my minister. In the first case I talked to the Clerk of the Privy Council about a particular problem with my minister. In the second instance I had a chance to talk to the Prime Minister at a social function. He asked me how it was going. I told him that I was having problems with my minister and said: `I have no time for this minister, I don't like him, please give me a new job.' The Prime Minister said: `I've got no time for your minister either, that's why you're there.' That is the best guidance I had ever been given — it kept me going for eighteen months."

Sometimes, deputy ministers deal with potential conflicts between the minister's interests and those of the Prime Minister by encouraging the minister to speak to the Prime Minister about a particular issue. In other situations they work with the Clerk of the Privy Council to reconcile differing views and perspectives. However, not every deputy minister balances these two accountability requirements successfully. On occasion deputy ministers who inform the Prime Minister about a minister's policy or administrative initiative lose the trust of the minister. In contrast, deputy ministers who fail to inform the Prime Minister or the Privy Council Office about a questionable ministerial decision shake the Prime Minister's confidence in them.

Ministers and deputy ministers can generally establish an understanding of their respective roles and resolve problems that could be caused by differing priorities or perceptions on the part of the minister and the Prime Minister. As one deputy minister explained:

"I guess I am ultimately accountable to the Prime Minister. It was emphasized in my case because my minister was not consulted about my appointment. When the crunch comes, my accountability is ultimately to the Prime Minister, but on a frequency basis it is more to the minister. My minister and I talked about this. He said that he understood this dual accountability to the minister and Prime Minister, but he told me that if I was ever going to go to the Prime Minister that I should tell him. I think that is very reasonable. I would never go to the Prime Minister without telling the minister. Usually, if it comes to that you don't have to go to the Prime Minister because everybody becomes reasonable."

There is no doubt that it is difficult to walk the tightrope between accountability to the minister and to the Prime Minister. Deputy ministers need wisdom and experience to do it well.

This concludes the discussion of the deputy minister's accountability to the Prime Minister. We now move on to the remaining relationships in Figure 1-1, the Public Service Commission and the Treasury Board. These two relationships are focused on the management component of the deputy minister's collective responsibilities.

3.3   THE DEPUTY MINISTER'S ACCOUNTABILITY TO THE PUBLIC SERVICE COMMISSION

The Public Service Commission (PSC) is an independent agency set up in the early 1900s to ensure a politically neutral public service.[3] The Public Service Employment Act (PSEA) of 1968 gives the PSC exclusive authority to make appointments in the public service, with some restrictions, and specifies that these appointments shall be made according to "merit" as determined by the Commission. The PSC is headed by three commissioners appointed for fixed terms. Like judges, they are removable only upon address of Parliament. The Commission reports annually to Parliament on its administration of the PSEA.

The Commission is authorized to delegate some of its staffing powers to deputy ministers. Normally, it does so. Deputy ministers are delegated authority to staff most positions in departments except for appointments to the senior management category and those involving entry to the public service. They may accept a resignation, declare a position abandoned, waive a probationary period or reject for cause a person on probation, and lay off personnel for lack of work. The authority delegated to deputy ministers is subject to PSC regulations.

HOW DO DEPUTY MINISTERS FULFIL THEIR ACCOUNTABILITY TO THE PSC?

Deputy ministers see their accountability to the Public Service Commission as straightforward. One deputy minister summed up the views expressed by most:

"Yes, I am accountable to the Public Service Commission because they delegate staffing authority to me and they try to hold me accountable to them for the exercise of that authority by various means such as audits. PSC could punish me by withdrawing my authority to staff, but that would be an extreme."

Deputy ministers satisfy the requirements of the Public Service Commission in two major ways: by ensuring that they have competent staff to help carry out the staffing function, and by maintaining informal relationships with the commissioners of the PSC and/or its senior executives.

To ensure that the department complies with PSC regulations, deputy ministers usually delegate staffing functions and the necessary legal authority to a director general or assistant deputy minister of personnel. The appropriate candidate for this job is someone who can maintain the confidence of the PSC, ensure that the department works within the regulations established by the PSC, and at the same time provide adequate support and services to the department. This delegation is subject to the approval of the PSC, so deputy ministers must have a senior personnel officer who is acceptable to the Commission.

Because the requirements of the PSC are usually well understood, deputy ministers do not spend much time on the staffing function. Their principal involvement with the PSC is in the areas of recruiting senior staff, establishing human resource priorities for the department, and managing major staffing changes such as downsizing or reorganization. Frequently, they deal personally with the commissioners and senior officials of the PSC. Deputy ministers said that previous experience in central agencies or with the PSC helped them to understand the perspectives and requirements of such agencies. One deputy minister who had a background in personnel said:

> *"I feel very close to the senior people of the central agencies. I know the Secretary of the Treasury Board and the Chairman of the PSC. I can grab the phone and talk to either one of them when I feel I have a problem."*

HIRING AND FIRING: A FRUSTRATION FOR MINISTERS

With the exception of their personal staff, ministers have no authority with respect to staffing. This authority structure is sometimes frustrating for ministers, particularly when they want to hire a specific person or they think someone is incompetent and should be dismissed. Ministers are responsible for the overall performance of a department, yet they cannot hire or dismiss staff. One deputy minister described the difficulties of reconciling the overall responsibilities of ministers with the specific authority of the PSC for staffing. This is presented in the box titled Hiring John Doe.

Deputy ministers seldom experience serious conflicts between accountability to the minister and accountability to the PSC. When a problem does emerge, it is very uncomfortable to be caught dangling between their accountability to the PSC, their accountability to the Prime Minister for collective management, and their obligations to the minister. It is essential that ministers and deputy ministers understand their respective roles and responsibilities in order to resolve such conflicts.

HOW THE PSC HOLDS DEPUTY MINISTERS ACCOUNTABLE

The PSC uses a variety of means to ensure that departments function within the limits of the Public Service Employment Act.

---   Annual Meetings Between the PSC Chairman and the Deputy Minister

The PSC Chairman and the Executive Director of Staffing meet annually with each deputy minister. These meetings are an important vehicle for communicating concerns about the department's staffing performance and provide an opportunity to discuss succession planning and the human resource priorities of the department. A major part of each meeting deals with the need to identify potential candidates for senior management positions.

Deputy ministers said they found these meetings very helpful in establishing a co-operative spirit between the department and the PSC and for providing an indication of PSC concerns about the department. Some deputy ministers said that as a result of such meetings they gave more attention to a problem or to the ongoing task of identifying and developing potential executives.

---   Meeting of the Commission with New Deputy Ministers

In addition to annual meetings with deputy ministers, the Chairman and Commissioners of the PSC meet with every newly appointed deputy minister. Their aim is to acquaint the deputy ministers with their responsibilities under the Public Service Employment Act.

---   Instruments of Delegation

The Chairman of the Commission requires each deputy minister upon appointment to sign an instrument of delegation, which is a statement acknowledging the responsibilities of the deputy minister under the Public Service Employment Act. An appendix to the instrument of delegation often identifies areas of staffing in the department that need improvement.

---   Feedback Reports to Departments

The PSC sends a semi-annual feedback report to deputy ministers. It is based on a statistical analysis of staffing actions and is intended to help the deputy minister monitor how the staffing process is operating.

HIRING JOHN DOE

"There was only one instance where I had a problem with the Minister on staffing. I intended to hire an assistant deputy minister and I looked around and talked to a lot of people. The Minister knew that I was undertaking this staffing action.

At one time the Minister observed to me that a person from a particular province was a pretty good guy. When I was in the final stages of the staffing process, I got a note from the Minister that he wanted to talk to me before I filled the job. I told the Minister that I had sorted through a lot of people and I was in the process of making an offer to John Doe. He said he didn't want John Doe appointed. He had come to the conclusion that John Doe was a supporter of another party. He believed John Doe was associated with a government of another party - even though the person had survived a change of government.

The Minister understood that I could go ahead and hire John Doe anyway. Later, I heard from his policy adviser that he was going to take it to the Prime Minister's Office. I wanted to avoid this if I could because we would both be losers. I knew that the Prime Minister and the Secretary to the Cabinet would probably support me and the Minister would be the loser, but that wouldn't be good for either of us.

So I decided to have another chat with the Minister. I told him that I hadn't given enough weight to his advice and his knowledge of the talents available for the department. I told him that if he had worries or reservations about John Doe, I would be willing to start the competition over. I told him that I had to do it this way rather than appoint someone else because the Public Service Commission would ask why I didn't hire John Doe, and I didn't want to say that the Minister made me do it. I also explained to him that if we hired John Doe and he didn't perform to both our expectations we would let him go.

The Minister then said I should go ahead and hire John Doe. He understood that if he pushed this much further with the Prime Minister's Office, it could be a headline in the paper. He backed off, and I gave him an indication that I would back off. We got along a lot better after that."

OBSERVATIONS

In this instance the deputy successfully dealt with the minister's concerns without compromising the staffing process. The expectation that the Prime Minister and the Clerk of the Privy Council, in addition to the Public Service Commission, would support the integrity of the staffing process illustrates the importance of the Prime Minister in establishing a framework of expectations with respect to the collective management of the Government.

—— Audits

The PSC conducts audits of departments to assess their performance and compliance with regulations.

—— PSC Retains Staffing Authority in Key Areas

Even though the PSC has delegated staffing authority for many classification levels to departments, it still staffs all senior management positions and retains staffing authority for recruitment and referral activities for entry into the public service.

—— Training and Promotion of Personnel Staff

The PSC controls the training of staffing officers and plays a key role in the appointment of senior managers of personnel functions.

—— Annual Report to Parliament

The PSC is responsible for reporting cases where deputy ministers or departments have not properly carried out their delegated responsibilities under the Public Service Employment Act or where delegation has been withdrawn. This is a powerful, but seldom needed, weapon; a negative report would likely cause a parliamentary committee to call the deputy minister and the PSC to testify.

—— Performance Appraisal of Deputy Ministers

Finally, as part of the performance appraisal of deputy ministers, the PSC submits to the Committee of Senior Officials (COSO) an evaluation of each deputy minister with respect to authorities delegated to the deputy minister under the Public Service Employment Act.

Overall, deputy ministers found that their accountability to the PSC was relatively clear and worked as effectively as could be expected given the cumbersome requirements of staffing legislation and regulations. There was widespread acceptance of the need for an independent agency to ensure that appointments in the public service are based on merit. Some deputy ministers were concerned about the division of responsibilities between the PSC and Treasury Board with respect to personnel management and career planning, as well as the length of time it takes to staff positions.

3.4   THE DEPUTY MINISTER'S ACCOUNTABILITY TO THE TREASURY BOARD

The Treasury Board is a statutory committee of ministers that receives staff support from the Treasury Board Secretariat and the Office of the Comptroller General.[4] The President of the Treasury Board is appointed by the Governor in Council on the recommendation of the Prime Minister. The Financial Administration Act establishes the legislative basis for the major functions of the Treasury Board with respect to the collective management of the government. The Treasury Board is used by the Prime Minister and Cabinet as an instrument for managing the public service[5]

Like other ministers, the President of the Treasury Board is accountable to the Prime Minister. One former Treasury Board President made this clear by saying:

"I am accountable to the Prime Minister and to Parliament in that order."

The Treasury Board is responsible for the following areas:

—— general administrative policy for the public service;

—— organization and establishment control;

—— financial management practices in the federal government;

—— the review of expenditure plans and determination of spending priorities;

—— personnel management, including compensation, classification, training, discipline;

—— negotiation of collective agreements and terms and conditions of employment;

—— implementation of priorities identified by the Government, such as downsizing or equalization of employment and advancement opportunities; and

—— improving management practices in the federal government.

As a statutory committee of ministers, the Treasury Board has certain decision-making powers with respect to such areas as departmental budget allocations and government-wide administrative policies. Thus, the Treasury Board establishes an overall collective management framework or set of constraints within which all ministers and departments have to operate.

HOW DOES THE TREASURY BOARD CARRY OUT ITS ROLE?

The Treasury Board, and by extension the Treasury Board Secretariat (TBS) and the Office of the Comptroller General (OCG), have a variety of general and specific means to exercise influence and to guide departments with respect to collective management.

—— Control of Estimates Process

The President of the Treasury Board, on behalf of the Government, submits the spending estimates to Parliament; the Treasury Board therefore manages the estimates process and is responsible for approving the vote structure and any allotment controls that are necessary.

—— Approval of Spending and Operational Plans

Spending plans are submitted to the Treasury Board, which decides on the level of funding for each department in relation to its programs and operational responsibilities. These decisions are made within the context of Cabinet direction.

—— Special Programs Controlled by Treasury Board

The Treasury Board is responsible for special programs such as official languages and affirmative action. To exercise this responsibility and ensure that government objectives are achieved, agreements with target objectives are negotiated with each department.

—— Pre-Transaction Controls

Treasury Board retains the right to give prior approval for specific actions by departments in certain areas. They include reorganizations involving the assistant deputy minister level; classifications involving the management category; letting contracts over specified dollar limits; and changes in charges or fees for public services.

—— Delegated Authorities

Treasury Board may delegate authorities in some areas. Under the Financial Administration Act, for example, the Board is responsible for classification. In discharging this responsibility the Board can delegate authority while providing standards for classifying positions, retaining control of designating classification officers, and conducting periodic audits of classified positions.

—— Guidelines/Functional Direction and Control

TBS and OCG provide a number of directives and guidelines to departments in areas such as financial management, internal audit, and program evaluation.

—— Reporting Requirements

Departments must comply with a number of reporting requirements in areas such as official languages, human resource planning, etc.

—— Administrative Regulations

The Treasury Board establishes overall government policies with respect to purchasing, property management and capital projects, as well as in a number of expenditure areas such as travel, use of taxis, computers, and training. In common service areas such as the purchase of supplies and property management, specific departments (e.g., the Department of Supply and Services and the Department of Public Works) are assigned responsibility for carrying out Treasury Board policies.

—— Performance Appraisal of Deputy Ministers
TBS and the Office of the Comptroller General submit an annual assessment of the performance of each department with respect to Treasury Board requirements to the Committee of Senior Officials, which evaluates the performance of deputy ministers.

The Treasury Board Secretariat relies on a variety of formal and informal methods to determine whether these policies and controls are being implemented. One important source of information is budget submissions and plans prepared by departments for Treasury Board approval. In addition, it relies on its own audits, departmental internal audits and evaluation reports, and audits by other agencies such as the Office of the Commissioner of Official Languages and the Office of the Auditor General. Finally, TBS staff can develop extensive knowledge about specific aspects of the operation of a department through meetings and discussions with departmental officials.

Although each source of information provides some indication of how departments are managing, deputy ministers said that if TBS staff do not have a good general knowledge of a department they can develop a highly fragmented view that does not take sufficient account of the overall management requirements of the department or of ministerial priorities.

ACCOUNTABILITY OF DEPUTY MINISTERS TO TREASURY BOARD

Deputy ministers said that their accountability to the Treasury Board is not as clear as their accountability to the Public Service Commission. Some recognized that by virtue of the Financial Administration Act they were accountable to the Treasury Board for certain delegated responsibilities, particularly in the area of personnel management. However, the majority described their role with respect to Treasury Board as a set of responsibilities that are part of the job of being a deputy minister and serving a minister. All recognized the need for the Treasury Board to perform the functions of employer and general manager of the public service. One deputy minister saw her accountability relationship with Treasury Board as follows:

"The accountability to my minister is in capitals, it's direct, it's continuing, intense and at times brutal. The relationship I feel to TBS, PSC, or PCO is of a different nature."

Deputy ministers recognize the importance of Treasury Board and the Treasury Board Secretariat in the collective management of government:

"I am not one to slam central agencies. If we didn't have central agencies, we'd rapidly invent them. Deputy ministers want to have a system of accountability."

However, deputy ministers both past and present expressed concerns about the way the Treasury Board often carries out its role:

"There is no question about it. Treasury Board has to be the general manager of government. There has got to be a general manager of government. But that doesn't mean nickel and dimeing departments."

They noted that the Treasury Board Secretariat tends to focus on specific functional areas or issues and does not provide much guidance on overall management requirements or support for department management objectives. There was some concern that the culture of the Treasury Board and its staff is biased towards criticizing and second-guessing departments as opposed to providing positive management support and direction. However, the overwhelming consensus among deputy ministers was that, on the whole, relationships with the Treasury Board and its Secretariat were much better now than they have been for several years.

In summary, deputy ministers have mixed views about the nature of their accountability to the Treasury Board. This is particularly noteworthy because Treasury Board has been a focal point for many accountability reforms over the past two decades.

THE COST OF CONTROL

The deputy minister's relationships with Treasury Board, the Public Service Commission, and other central agencies deal with the more visible and tangible aspects of government, such as staffing, financial administration, and contracting. Consequently, they have been the subject of a great deal of scrutiny over the years by politicians, officials, royal commissions, and others. One result of all this attention is that in terms of day-to-day management of resources, the responsibilities of deputy ministers are reasonably well defined and understood. A less desirable result is the complex web of controls and regulations that has evolved, complete with watchdog agencies.

In the past 20 years the institutional environment within which departments work has changed dramatically with the addition or expansion of several agencies that review the activities of departments and issue public reports on their performance.[6] These developments include the creation of the Office of the Commissioner of Official Languages in 1970; the creation of the Canadian Human Rights Commission in 1976-77; the expanded mandate given to the Office of the Auditor General in 1977; and the establishment of Information and Privacy Commissioners in 1982.

Central agencies of the federal government were expanded during the 1970s and early 1980s. The Office of the Comptroller General, which reports to the President of the Treasury Board, assumed responsibility for improving management practices in the federal government and developing program evaluation and internal audit capabilities in departments. In addition, two new central agencies were created in the late 1970s and early '80s (and abolished in 1984), the Ministry of State for Social Development and the Ministry of State for Economic and Regional Development.

Deputy ministers feel that, in many cases, controls unduly restrict their freedom to manage. The final sections of this chapter describe how deputy ministers deal with the complexity of formal controls and how they feel about the ultimate effect of such measures on their accountability.

3.5 MANAGING THE COMPLEXITY: THE INFORMAL SYSTEM

The functions performed by the Public Service Commission, Treasury Board Secretariat, the Privy Council Office and COSO establish a collective management framework for controlling the Government's budget and personnel resources and achieving government-wide priorities. However, deputy ministers and central agency staff point out that the formal systems or machinery are lubricated by important informal processes.

Deputy ministers and central agency staff agree that departments with a good track record and reputation are treated differently from departments with a poor management record. By holding up approval of submissions or deferring consideration of proposed expenditures until they have satisfied themselves as to the facts of a submission, TBS can exert considerable influence and give relatively clear signals to a department about its performance.

In many instances there is considerable informal communication between TBS and deputy ministers or other senior officials before expenditure proposals are submitted for approval or when reorganizations are planned. This enables the Treasury Board Secretariat and the department to understand their respective requirements. In addition, in some instances departments take great care to explain their circumstances to senior officials in the Treasury Board Secretariat and obtain exceptions or elicit understandings about how certain regulations will be implemented. Similar communication occurs between deputy ministers and the staff of the Privy Council Office and the Public Service Commission.

> *"How do central agencies hold me to account? I've had meetings with them, especially on department management issues as well as on how we apply legislation. I dislike thinking of central agencies as bodies. They are groups of people."*

> *"The relationship I feel to TBS/PSC/PCO is more in terms of a supporting nature. I've been able to go to the Treasury Board Secretariat for advice and help."*

> *"There is always a certain degree of creative tension between the Treasury Board and the departments and a certain amount of kibitzing between TBS analysts and department officials. But, I know that if there is a problem, I can take it to the Secretary of the Treasury Board and we can have a reasonable dialogue on it."*

One informal process that makes it possible for central agencies and departments to work within this complex structure is what one deputy minister called the 'personalization' of the roles of the Secretary of the Treasury Board and the Chairman of the Public Service Commission. By making themselves available to deputy ministers to discuss problems, the heads of TBS and the PSC can make the adjustments that enable deputy ministers to meet ministerial and department management requirements in the context of the collective management framework. Similarly, the staff of the Privy Council Office hold frequent discussions with departmental staff concerning government priorities and submissions to Cabinet.

In recent years communication between departments and central agencies has been improved by regular meetings between deputy ministers and senior representatives of central agencies. The Clerk of the Privy Council meets each week with all deputy ministers to discuss the Government's agenda for that week. The Secretary of the Treasury Board often meets with deputy ministers to discuss management concerns, and the Chairman of the Public Service Commission meets annually with each deputy minister with respect to staffing. In addition, the Associate Secretary to the Cabinet for Senior Appointments now meets with newly-appointed deputy ministers to discuss their functions and the collective management concerns of the Government. Deputy ministers found these meetings useful, both as a source of guidance and advice and as a mechanism to resolve outstanding problems between departments and central agencies.

The importance of these types of meetings for defining collective management concerns was illustrated by three deputy ministers:

> "I was given a little bit of an agenda — mainly by the Secretary of the Treasury Board. He said there are two things you should really get under control — the financial management and the degree of overlap between functions. I also briefed the Secretary on downsizing. I made him very much aware of what I was doing. I knew what they were trying to accomplish and I made sure they knew what I was doing."

> "I met with the Secretary of the Treasury Board shortly after I arrived here. He said, `You know, you have a problem with one program'. And, he was right, I did. It is this interaction between the Treasury Board and the department that provides direction."

> "When I came here the first person to invite me to lunch was the Secretary of the Treasury Board. He said, `In my list of problem departments, yours is No. 1 or No. 2'. Shortly after that I saw a Treasury Board submission prepared by the department that was terrible and I knew what he was concerned about. The Department was just going to Treasury Board for more money every time they had a problem. I made one of my major priorities improving this relationship with Treasury Board by getting our house in order."

The informal system thus depends on the sensitivity of central agency officials to the problems faced by departments and the knowledge and appreciation by deputy ministers and department staff of the concerns and objectives of central agencies. At the same time, the informal system is extremely important for making the complex collective management structure work. One deputy minister felt so strongly about this he said:

> "The informal network should not be sneezed at as the old boys' network; it is the arterial system, it is the heart and blood of the system, and it is what makes the system work."

One reason why informal communication is so important is that deputy ministers are relatively isolated from one another on a day-to-day basis; they need some means to seek advice or obtain feedback on overall government priorities. Deputy ministers have weekly meetings with their colleagues and the Clerk of Privy Council, annual sessions with the heads of central agencies, and specific meetings with other deputy ministers to deal with interdepartmental problems. Other than these relatively formal occasions, deputy ministers spend most of their time working on departmental issues. There is little encouragement or opportunity for deputy ministers to meet informally on issues of common concern.

3.6   LIMITS TO ACCOUNTABILITY FOR COLLECTIVE MANAGEMENT

The accountability system for deputy ministers with respect to collective management has been successful in maintaining a staffing system based on merit; ensuring that deputy ministers work towards government objectives and priorities; implementing improved management systems and practices throughout the federal government; and maintaining day-to-day policy co-ordination between departments. These achievements have not been without costs in terms of increasing the complexity of the system. There are also major limitations on the extent to which central direction can be provided to deputy ministers and departments in an organization as large and complex as the federal public service.

BALANCING CENTRAL CONTROLS WITH DEPARTMENT MANAGEMENT

For Cabinet government to function effectively, deputy ministers must be accountable for collective management functions; that is, for achieving overall government priorities and meeting government-wide management standards. At the same time, however, the collective management structure must allow deputy ministers to manage departments in a way that supports the minister's needs and takes into account the specific requirements and the unique characteristics of each department.

As the Privy Council Office noted in its submission to the Royal Commission on Financial Management and Accountability (Lambert Commission) in 1979, it is difficult to achieve this balance.

"... in every functional area in the personnel system the deputy head is required to work in conjunction with at least one other agency. In no instance does the deputy head have the statutory mandate for any element of the personnel system. The present system places managerial responsibility with deputies and yet managerial authority is vested in either the Treasury Board or the Public Service Commission. While the Commission has a role to play in the allocation of resources, the deputy minister must have the necessary authority commensurate with his responsibilities. His accountability to his minister and to the public service as a whole is based on his performance which, in large part, is a function of his ability to recruit and motivate people to do the tasks required. The protection of the probity for the staffing process and the interests of co-ordinated central management should be properly balanced against the deputy's need to manage his own resources and to be held accountable for them." [7]

In response to concerns that the federal government was moving too far in the direction of central controls, the Privy Council Office recommended:

> "... a balance must be struck between the individual responsibility of the deputy to manage his department and his collective responsibility for effective and efficient management of the public service as a whole. The use of management standards and guidelines as control measures should decline. As past experience has shown, controls have never been a suitable substitute for accountability." [8]

The warnings of the Privy Council Office went largely unheeded in the period from 1979 to 1983. In response to concerns expressed by the Auditor General concerning financial control and program management, as well as the recommendations of the Royal Commission on Financial Management and Accountability in 1979, the federal government initiated a number of central management changes and controls that aggravated the problem of how to balance the collective management priorities with department management requirements.

By 1983 these changes had reached the point where one of the principal proponents of central systems, the Auditor General, was concerned that central controls and management processes had gone too far and that they were undermining productive management and the accountability of deputy ministers. In a chapter entitled "Constraints to Productive Management in the Public Service" in his 1983 Annual Report, the Auditor General echoed some of the original concerns of the Privy Council Office.[9]

The Auditor General's report suggested that to achieve productive management, the Government should undertake "selective deregulation" by reducing constraints where possible; adapting central rules and regulations to the operational requirements of departments; giving departments more authority; and making departments more accountable for results.

The Auditor General highlighted a continuing dilemma faced by the federal government. In order to co-ordinate their activities, achieve consistent management standards and pursue special priorities, governments tend to develop government-wide rules and regulations, approval processes, special agencies, or expanded central agency responsibilities. New controls or regulations are often a response to public pressures or disclosure of a particular problem, with little concern for the implications for overall management of departments. In the guise of increasing economy or efficiency for a number of individual areas, deputy ministers become less and less able to carry out overall management of the department. Eventually, the management of departments may become so cumbersome that it is difficult for deputy ministers to help ministers achieve their priorities within a reasonable time.

DIFFUSED AND FRAGMENTED ACCOUNTABILITY

The consensus among deputy ministers and many central agency executives was that the ultimate result of extensive central controls and approval processes is diffused accountability. They noted that once central agencies become an integral part of the management process of departments, deputy ministers can no longer be held accountable. One deputy minister explained the problem of holding deputy ministers accountable from a Treasury Board perspective.

> *"Perhaps one of the reasons there doesn't appear to be an exacting accounting taking place between departments and Treasury Board is that there are so many controls over processes that central agencies become part of the decision making. This means that there cannot be an exacting that takes place because potential problems are taken care of before they emerge. This helps to avoid government embarrassments but it confuses the accountability relationship."*

Deputy ministers generally accepted the complexity of the collective management structure as necessary and inevitable. Their major task was to learn how to manage within this institutional framework. However, many still had concerns about complex and fragmented accountability and responsibility.

> *"I am concerned that I have so many accountabilities that I am accountable to none. At one extreme there are so many players involved that there is a danger that something will fall between the cracks. On the other hand, I am concerned that I am accountable to so many that in fact the role that I'm expected to play can be impaired. I am concerned about ending up with a system where deputies are structurally crucified."*

> *"There is no one organization that takes cognizance of the overall performance of a department. Thus deputy ministers are faced with answering to the fragmented, unco-ordinated demands of several different agencies. The deputy minister may be severely (and publicly) criticized for his failure to meet bilingualism goals, while the overall performance and efficiency of the department goes unnoticed. Because of this problem a specific line of accountability is not achieved."*

> *"My point of extreme frustration is that Treasury Board never really accepts your affirmative action plan or indicates that you have satisfactory policy or programs in these areas. They don't accept any responsibility or obligation to the department in accomplishing such objectives. They want 100 per cent of every*

objective and then they are still not happy with it. Nobody will say we accept that as right, nor will they share the risk with me as in the corporate private sector."

"Accountability for me is to get the best of an individual associated with running a department. It should not be a one-way street. It should be a reciprocal relationship. That reciprocity does not happen between departments and central agencies. They hold me accountable for achieving their various objectives, but they do not try to mesh these with my department's objectives. The accountability is very piecemeal. It is like painting with dots. By putting all sorts of dots and holes on a piece of paper, you are supposed to make a picture."

SUBSTITUTING RULES FOR RESPONSIBILITY AND PROCESSES FOR PERFORMANCE

Because central agencies concentrate on having deputy ministers achieve specific targets or follow specified management practices, most deputy ministers do not feel accountable to central agencies for the overall management of the department. They identified a tendency to substitute rules for responsibility and management processes for performance and productivity. Two factors underlie this view.

First, most deputy ministers felt that few people in central agencies understand the overall management requirements of their departments; as a result they are not able to judge the overall performance of departments. Deputy ministers pointed out that each department had specific and unique management requirements, a particular clientele, individual operational requirements and, most important, particular ministerial objectives and priorities. These facets of the department have to be understood before central agency staff can really appreciate or assess the overall performance of a deputy minister or a department.

Second, deputy ministers said that the staff of central agencies are functional specialists and tend to concentrate on their limited area of expertise. Their job is to achieve a particular purpose (with respect to, for example, official languages, staffing, classification, organization, administrative policy), but they are not mandated specifically to concern themselves with the overall management of a department or its responsiveness and support to a minister. One deputy minister summed up the concerns of many deputy ministers:

"There is too much concern for detail and not enough concern with the larger picture of good managing."

To cope with the complex and specialized demands of central groups while leaving enough time to support the minister's priorities, deputy ministers have to rely on functional experts within the department.

They usually delegate key functions and liaison with central agencies to assistant deputy ministers or directors general of finance, personnel, administration, audit and evaluation, and planning. These individuals are responsible to the deputy minister for ensuring that the department works within guidelines and regulations established by central agencies. They ensure that proposals and submissions are in a form acceptable to central agencies.

These departmental staff functions are often performed by people with expertise in a functional or professional area but with limited knowledge of the operations of the department. To maintain credibility with central agencies, such staff may be more demanding about central agency requirements than the central agencies themselves. Deputy ministers said that they had to be careful to ensure that staff functions supported the requirements and priorities of the minister and department as well as collective management requirements. If not, fragmented demands from outside the department could be amplified by persons within the department.

Despite some concerns about the complexity of the accountability system, deputy ministers did not think that major changes in the roles of the Treasury Board, the Public Service Commission or the Privy Council Office would help. In fact, there was strong consensus that the federal government had undertaken too many institutional changes over the past decade. The main challenge now is to give departments enough stability and flexibility to enable them to support ministers and meet the challenge of downsizing the public service.

3.7   RECENT REFORMS: INCREASING DEPARTMENT ACCOUNTABILITY AND RESPONSIBILITY

A change occurred between 1983 and 1987 in the way in which deputy ministers viewed central agencies. The elimination of two co-ordinating agencies in 1984, the Ministry of State for Social Development and the Ministry of State for Economic and Regional Development, was viewed as an important step in reducing burdensome central agency decision-making processes. Deputy ministers said that their relationships with central agencies are more positive and supportive than they were previously.

One of the beneficial effects of downsizing in the public service has been to provide an agreed resource framework for departments and to encourage the Treasury Board and departments to focus more on results and efficiency than on management procedures. One deputy minister, who admitted that he had been a strong critic of central agencies in the early 1980s, said:

> "I think that there have been changes in Treasury Board, the PSC and PCO. There is a mood to help. In the mid-seventies, the more surprise you could get in a Cabinet document the better. The idea was to jump-start the process and get it through before other ministers could figure out what you were doing. So you had Treasury Board trying to ride herd on this situation. It is now viewed as bad behaviour to surprise people. It is the convention that you consult and co-operate. The PCO polices this by ensuring that various departments have their inputs into Cabinet documents. I think that there has been a change over time in the level of detailed control. There has definitely been a change in the consultation practices of the Treasury Board. There is more flexibility for the deputy minister and responsibility has increased. However, there is a long way to go yet."

The remainder of this section deals with the Increased Ministerial Authority and Accountability process, which is the responsibility of the Treasury Board.

IMAA: CAN THIS INITIATIVE LEAD TO IMPROVED ACCOUNTABILITY?

The Increased Ministerial Authority and Accountability (IMAA) regime was announced by the Treasury Board in 1986. Most deputy ministers we interviewed supported the principles of IMAA, observing that the changes in central agency reporting and approval requirements introduced as part of IMAA were a welcome relief from the burden of central agency controls.[10]

Despite the positive tone of deputy ministers regarding their accountability to central agencies, we found that the federal government still faces significant challenges in implementing the spirit of IMAA. IMAA involves a major change in the role of the Treasury Board Secretariat. Once IMAA is implemented it is expected that Treasury Board will be more concerned with what departments achieve in terms of program results and service-wide policy objectives and less concerned with how well procedural rules are followed.

A Treasury Board document published in December 1987 explained the role of IMAA this way:

> "In 1986, the Government adopted a new philosophy of management that relies more on the ability of managers to manage and less on detailed regulations. This will gradually change the way Treasury Board fulfils its mandate, providing individual ministers and senior management with greater authority, and making them more clearly accountable for the good management of their departments and agencies." [11]

IMAA is intended to improve overall efficiency by streamlining control measures and reducing some of the requirements for reports to Treasury Board. Several longstanding constraints to productive management are removed, and ministers have greater authority to reallocate financial and human resources.[12] For example, ministers and departments are given increased authority to approve competitive contracts, authorize special pay assignments, and implement administrative policies such as those governing attendance at conferences, per diem pay rates for consultants, and so on.

IMAA presents several major opportunities for improving the accountability relationship between the Treasury Board and departments (i.e., ministers and deputy ministers):

—— It clearly recognizes the fundamental and important accountability relationship between ministers and deputy ministers with respect to departmental management through joint signature of a memorandum of understanding between the department and Treasury Board. The process of negotiation and review of the memorandum of understanding can help ministers and deputy ministers develop a common understanding of their roles and responsibilities in managing the department within the context of collective management responsibilities;

—— It establishes a clear understanding between Treasury Board and the minister and deputy minister with respect to their mutual responsibilities and provides the flexibility to adjust those expectations annually. Therefore, it clarifies the accountability of ministers and deputy ministers by distinguishing clearly between what departments are responsible for and what the Treasury Board is responsible for;

—— It recognizes that the collective management requirements of Treasury Board must be tailored to each department and provides opportunities for departments to suggest or initiate changes to central regulations that increase productivity;

—— It encourages the various functional areas in Treasury Board and individual departments (e.g., personnel, finance, evaluation, audit, administrative policy, classification) to focus on the requirements of managing the department as opposed to meeting government-wide standards and priorities; and

—— It reduces some of the burden of controls and information requirements that have blurred the accountability of deputy ministers and limited the authority of ministers and deputy ministers to manage departments.

PITFALLS AND TRAPS FOR IMAA

IMAA follows a long history of attempted reforms that have met with limited success, including the planning, programming and budgeting system (PPBS) introduced in the late 1960s and early 1970s; management by objectives; A-base reviews; operational performance measurement systems; and strategic plans. These and other management innovations were heralded as panaceas but quickly ran out of steam in the implementation process. Many of these earlier initiatives were based on private sector notions of management that assumed that clear objectives could be specified for programs and that administration could be carried out as if politics, ministers and elections did not exist.

The major challenge facing IMAA is to avoid the trap of equating successful performance by deputy ministers with the achievement of central agency management standards, rather than with effective support of the minister and overall management of the department. It will be difficult to avoid bureaucratizing the process to the point where ministers feel that it is solely the deputy minister's responsibility. Given the turnover among ministers and deputy ministers, it will be tricky to obtain the full benefit from the memoranda of understanding based on three-year cycles. Finally, it will be important for Treasury Board to review the activities of departments and consider administrative policies in light of the management challenges faced by departments. Chapter 7 sets out some of the conditions that must be met by the Treasury Board, the Treasury Board Secretariat and departments if they are to implement IMAA successfully.[13]

3.8 FINDINGS: ACCOUNTABILITY FOR COLLECTIVE MANAGEMENT

The accountability system for collective management is complex and has high potential for conflict, but deputy ministers can usually balance their multiple accountability requirements to the Prime Minister, the Public Service Commission and the Treasury Board with their accountability to the minister. To a large extent, achieving the federal government's collective management objectives depends on the following factors:

—— the judgement exercised by deputy ministers in finding ways to reconcile conflicting demands in the collective management process;

—— acknowledgement by deputy ministers of the role of central agencies and the necessity to respond to their requirements;

—— sensitivity of central agency staff to departmental management requirements; and

—— maintenance of the extensive informal links that have developed between departments and central agencies.

There are limits to increasing the accountability of deputy ministers through central agency controls and regulations. Deputy ministers recognize that some collective management functions must be carried out by central agencies. They know that they have to play an active role in determining and reconciling collective management requirements with the priorities of the minister and the management needs of the department. However, extensive central agency controls lead to fragmented and diffused demands on deputy ministers. They make it difficult for deputy ministers to be responsive to ministers. They reduce the ability of deputy ministers to use their experience and judgement. The more central agencies regulate the activities of departments in specific areas, the less able is the government to hold deputy ministers meaningfully accountable for the overall management of departments.

Recent initiatives to increase the authority of ministers and deputy ministers to manage departments are positive steps towards improving the accountability of deputy ministers for department and collective management by making their accountability more realistic. The problem from the point of view of deputy ministers is that while they are accountable to many different people for specific aspects of their performance, there is not much emphasis on their overall performance in managing the department to achieve ministerial priorities and collective management requirements. Deputy ministers want to be more accountable for the management of their departments as long as they have more authority to manage key resources. They want central agencies to understand the constraints, opportunities and challenges they face.

The IMAA initiative by Treasury Board and recent efforts by the PSC and PCO to meet with deputy ministers and to reach greater understanding on common concerns and priorities are important improvements. These efforts should enhance the ability of deputy ministers to balance ministerial and departmental priorities with collective management concerns.

CHAPTER **4** # MANAGING THE MINISTER'S AGENDA

T he accountability relationships described in the foregoing chapters provide a context within which ministers and deputy ministers may carry out their roles. The application of these relationships may change somewhat from one department to the next but their essential nature remains constant across the government.

Each department, however, has a different set of responsibilities. Even within the same department, priorities and problems change over time, and often overnight. Ministers must take the current set of responsibilities, priorities, and other considerations and come up with a plan of action. This plan is normally referred to as the minister's agenda.[1]

Agenda-setting is critical to ensuring that deputy ministers are responsive to ministers and the Government. A clear ministerial agenda enables deputy ministers to ensure that the department is responsive to ministerial direction. In this chapter we explore how different ministers set and implement their agendas and how deputy ministers demonstrate their accountability to ministers and the Government by assisting them. We begin the chapter with a description of the background against which agenda-setting decisions are made.

4.1 THE AGENDA-SETTING ENVIRONMENT

The environment in which ministers set their agendas is complex and uncertain. It is marked by high levels of diversity and interdependence among players in the agenda-setting process. By diversity, we mean the wide range of interests and goals held by individuals, groups, and institutions. Interdependence arises from the existence of important linkages between the players. These varied interests and interconnections mean that it is difficult for ministers to know at any particular time which issues to pursue, who will support pursuing them, and how the issue might affect others in the environment.

To complicate matters even further, ministers have very little real power over most of those who play a part in setting and implementing their agendas. Thus, on issues which require negotiation, cooperation or reconcilation of competing interests, the capacity of ministers and their deputy ministers to find workable solutions is limited to their ability to influence the players involved.[2] This creates a high degree of uncertainty for ministers in regard to selecting (and later implementing) an agenda, as well as for deputy ministers in assisting them.

The uncertainty in the environment is aggravated by the public nature and rapid pace of the political process. At any time a seemingly innocent issue can gain national importance because of media interest, pressure from the opposition or the activities of an interest group. Increased news coverage, access to the media by various groups and the prevalence of television have "accelerated the pace of politics. Governments no longer control the news agenda as they once did."[3] As a result, it is difficult for governments and ministers to set and manage an agenda through to completion. The focus of the media and interest groups on the immediate issues of the day may make it difficult for ministers to concern themselves with longer-term goals. As one deputy minister said:

"I spent the major part of my first six months dealing with an unanticipated crisis issue. I had a very hard time finding the hours in the day to devote to what I perceived as the major function of my department."

In this section we review the major factors that affect agenda-setting in this complex environment. We start with the broad government context, then move to the working level of the minister and deputy minister.

THE GOVERNMENT AGENDA

On taking office, governments face many expectations. If they are to achieve a credible record during their term of office they must establish a limited number of objectives that can be accomplished during the time available. It is these objectives that become their priorities and form the government's agenda. They are announced in statements by the Prime Minister or in the Speech from the Throne.

Governments define their objectives in two ways. The first is by outlining a set of values, norms or attitudes. Recent examples would be national reconciliation or the emphasis on the private sector as the means to encourage economic growth. The second is by identifying specific agenda items, such as free trade, deficit reduction, tax reform, or patriation of the constitution. These two kinds of direction provide an overall context within which ministerial agendas may be set. Figure 4-1 illustrates the players involved in government agenda setting.

To establish an agenda for a particular department a minister has to understand where the department and its proposed initiatives fit within the context of the many competing objectives vying for attention

FIGURE 4-1

THE GOVERNMENT
AGENDA-SETTING PROCESS

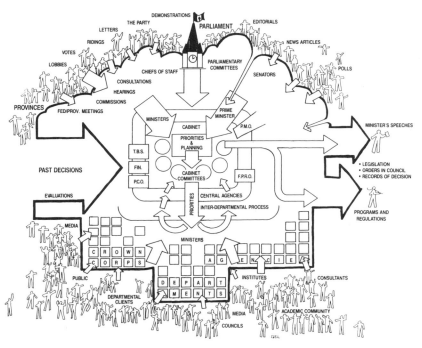

G. MILNE/L. TYLER
Nepean Development Consultants, Ottawa

and support of the Cabinet and the Prime Minister.[4] The Prime Minister plays a central role in determining which issues form the Government's agenda by controlling appointments, managing changes in the machinery of government, and appointing the chairpersons and members of the various Cabinet committees. In addition, the Prime Minister influences the agenda by virtue of his public role as spokesman for the Government and the party. Therefore, ministers must ensure that their initiatives are consistent with the priorities of the Prime Minister and the Government.

AT THE DEPARTMENT LEVEL: MANAGING IN AN HOURGLASS

Ministers and deputy ministers can be seen as sharing the neck of an hourglass in agenda-setting. In a typical department ministers and deputy ministers must balance downward pressure from the Prime Minister and Cabinet, lateral pressure from Parliament and a variety of agencies and groups, and upward pressures from the department. All of these forces converge at the neck of the hourglass and must be reconciled or otherwise dealt with. Figure 4-2 illustrates this environment.

Pressures for government initiatives can emerge from within or outside the government. The opposition parties advocate new approaches to problems such as unemployment or regional disparities. Parliamentary committees advocate revised policies. The caucus of the party in power pushes for favourite initiatives or fulfilment of campaign promises. Provincial governments press for changes in policies or funding in their fields of interest. Some interest groups argue for increased expenditures while others argue for reduced spending and lower taxes.

Within the public service, officials press for program modifications or initiatives to respond to their perceptions of new needs or problems. Central agencies push for improved management practices. In many cases coalitions of interests are formed around particular problems, solutions or opportunities.[5] Loosely-connected groups of officials, clients, interest groups and sometimes Cabinet ministers press for policy or resource allocation changes or modifications in regulations and legislation. This process is evident daily in newspaper accounts of fishermen, cultural groups, farmers or industry associations pressing governments and ministers for change.

The requirements of ministerial responsibility in the Parliamentary and Cabinet system of government and the nature of the political process make it difficult for ministers and deputy ministers to delegate

FIGURE 4-2

THE MINISTER'S AGENDA SETTING PROCESS

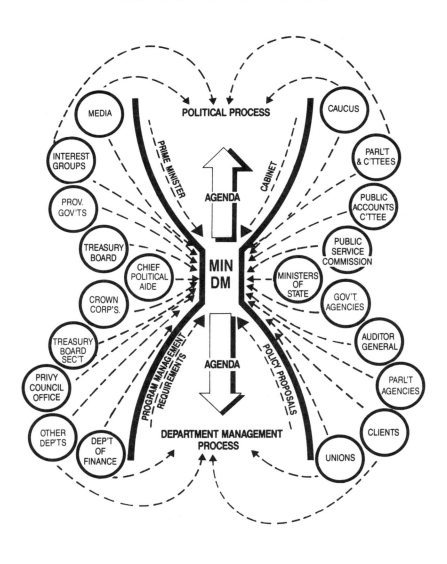

their agenda-setting functions. Many questions that ministers must deal with involve subtle judgements and difficult trade-offs between competing objectives, as well as careful attention to parliamentary concerns and the overall priorities of the Government and outside agencies. Two deputy ministers expressed the difficulties this way:

> *"It is not too difficult to figure out expectations. I knew pretty well what they were. The problem was reconciliation of divergent expectations from many different groups."*

> *"I get different signals from different sources. The PM tells my minister that program X is important and deserves resources. However, when I go to the DMs of central agencies they say, `Well sure this is a priority, you can devote as many of your own resources to this as you want.' The problem I have is who to believe. Everything is a priority. We are trying to divert diverted funds, so new priorities have to come out of something."*

From their vantage point at the focus of these competing pressures, the minister and deputy minister are usually the best placed to appreciate the total context in which an issue must be considered. This places enormous pressures on the two people in the neck of the hourglass. Deputy ministers used a variety of analogies to describe the uncertainties of their environment.

> *"The job of a deputy minister is like a spider trying to spin a web in a toilet bowl. Every time you are close to being finished, a flush would destroy it."*

> *"To characterize my environment at the department: when I was driving to work each morning, I would wonder which 3 bricks would fall on my head that day. In any given week, I would have at least 15 bricks fall, but it had been a good week if, as I was driving home on the Friday evening, I could say to myself that I had been able to identify at least half of them in advance."*

> *"I have the impression that I am juggling a large number of balls in the air and the trick is not to drop any. It is not the big policy balls that cause the problems — they have a net under them. It is the little ones (like a contract) that cause you problems. In a large and complex department, this means disasters can occur deep down in the organization."*

Despite the great difficulty involved in agenda setting, deputy ministers and ministers alike indicated that it was essential to have a clear agenda if they were to accomplish anything in the context of these multiple pressures. The views of one deputy minister summed up the views of other deputies:

> *"If you don't drive the department with priorities and an agenda, it drifts. All sorts of ideas will perk up, but few will actually get done."*

4.2 THE MINISTER'S AGENDA

The minister's personal agenda is the set of initiatives, policies or program changes to which he or she gives priority for a period of a few months to about two years. It could include downsizing the department, eliminating programs or initiatives such as the National Energy Program, issuing a white paper on national defence, or changing the National Transportation Act.

Ministers find it essential to have a clear agenda. One minister explained:

"The most important task of a minister is to set an agenda for himself and the department. I used to think that a minister should just make sure that the Government didn't do too much to screw things up further. After my first experience as a minister I became convinced that if you don't have an agenda, someone else will make one for you. People expect a government or a department to do something. You cannot leave a vacuum."

Several ministers commented that each department has specific legislative duties and many longstanding traditions that influence or even shape the agenda. Ministers find that they are charged with a public trust or responsibility for key government functions, such as the health of Canadians, the integrity of the justice system or the safety of the transportation system. Ministers are expected to provide for the proper stewardship of departments and ensure that their basic functions and program obligations are fulfilled. For example, if they are not able to ensure that statutory payments are delivered on a timely basis to the unemployed, pensioners or veterans, they are criticized by parliamentarians, clients and the press. If they do not administer the immigration process equitably or ensure that the tax system is administered fairly, they face tough questions about the exercise of their responsibilities.

HOW MINISTERS SET THEIR AGENDAS

Ministers balance four major pressures in the process of determining priorities: the need to work within the overall political process and priorities of the Government; the requirement to observe resource and legislative constraints; the pressure to respond to a variety of groups within and outside the government; and the necessity of formulating an agenda that recognizes the minister's responsibilities to carry out existing departmental obligations and requirements with respect to policies and programs. The approach they take in establishing an agenda that responds to these pressures may depend on their interests, the agenda of the previous minister, the government's agenda, the advice provided by the deputy minister, and the need to respond to particular events or emerging problems.

We encountered four types of ministerial approaches to agenda-setting: ministers who come with their own agendas; ministers who accept and implement the Government agenda or a previous minister's agenda; ministers who develop their agenda after arriving in the department; and ministers who operate with no agenda.

Ministers who come with their own agenda   Based on comments by ministers, 15 to 20 per cent of ministers arrive with an agenda and know what they want to do when they are appointed to a portfolio. In most cases these ministers are familiar with the policy field, having had business experience in that area or having been the opposition critic for that department. In other cases, ministers knew well in advance that they would be appointed to a particular portfolio and had the time to develop an agenda consistent with the party's priorities. These quotations explain this particular approach to agenda-setting:

> *"The minister had been given a pretty fair indication regarding the portfolio that he would be given if he won the election. He had his agenda ready a full year before he was sworn in as minister. While he was in opposition, the minister had his own study done of a policy issue. He knew the issue at least as well as the officials when he got to office."*

> *"The minister had a pre-approved mandate from the Prime Minister which was broadly supported by the Government. He did not have to go through the approval process with his colleagues. As a result soon after the minister arrived, we were in a position to implement his priorities."*

> *"When I arrived as minister, the department had prepared a policy paper for me which reflected speeches that I had made and the party platform. I thought some-one had read my mind. It was a very helpful document for providing a sense of direction for the department and a philosophical base for me. It also had a major impact on my level of confidence in the deputy minister and the department."*

When ministers arrive with an agenda, the major role of deputy ministers is to help them translate it into specific programs or initiatives that could be implemented by the department. They advise ministers on how to achieve their priorities within the context of government priorities, the functions of other departments, the requirements established by Treasury Board, and the requirements of the Cabinet decision-making process. The mandate case, presented later in this chapter, is an example of this type of agenda-setting.

Ministers who implement the Government agenda or the agenda of a previous minister   Ministers appointed after a major policy change, when legislative, budgetary and organizational proposals are well under way, may simply assume the existing agenda and see to its implementation. In other instances a minister may be appointed specifically to carry out a portion of the Government agenda. Soon after their arrival these ministers may be called upon to advance proposals at Cabinet committees, defend policy initiatives in the House of Commons and negotiate with other ministers to implement or fulfil commitments made by a previous minister. There is often little room for the minister's own priorities or concerns until the inherited priorities have been dealt with. About 15 to 20 per cent of ministers face this situation.

One minister explained that the previous minister had started so many policy initiatives and raised so many expectations that he felt it necessary to concentrate on delivering on those promises. It is often more difficult for a minister to carry out the agenda of a previous minister or to focus on management questions than to initiate new policy changes. The press, for example, may observe that a particular minister has no agenda or has not done anything different from the previous minister. Ministers in this situation may have clear agendas, but the components are not as visible or newsworthy as new programs, policies or legislation.

Two chief political aides explained how their ministers assumed existing agendas.

> "There were several task forces going on when we got to this department. For the first few months there were bombs going off all over the place. These things determined our initial agenda."

> "The agenda was largely set while we were in opposition and it was part of the party platform. The minister could not deviate too much from it."

In these situations the role of the deputy minister is to help the minister link his or her initiatives to the overall priorities of the Government, or to assist in defending, promoting and implementing policies established by a previous minister.

Ministers who develop an agenda after arriving in the department   The third type of agenda-setting is probably the most common, representing perhaps 30 to 35 per cent of cases. With frequent Cabinet shuffles, ministers may have no immediate idea of what priorities to pursue in their new department. If their predecessors have left considerable room to manoeuvre and the Government agenda provides only general policy direction, ministers are freer to set their own agenda.

Ministers in this situation spend a lot of time in their first few months trying to decide what they want to do. They meet with their political advisers; discuss various alternatives and proposals with the deputy minister; read department briefings; meet with clients and interest groups; and meet with their colleagues and caucus.

These ministers may adopt agenda items proposed by deputy ministers and departments or seek additional advice from chief political aides or outside advisers. The following quotations illustrate how various ministers went about this task:

> "The minister can push certain priorities or the deputy minister can push. If you can have a good blending of the political and the bureaucratic priorities, that is good. The best outcomes are when the blend is good between both."

> "The way to determine priorities is for the minister to come into the department, ask a lot of questions, listen to the advice of the department and some outside groups and choose three or four things that he can do that are politically right and which are right for the department as well as for the Government and himself."

This type of agenda-setting requires extensive discussion between the minister and the deputy minister. The role of the deputy minister is to help the minister become familiar with the department and its basic needs and to provide a range of possible actions or initiatives that reflect the interests of the minister. It requires a high degree of sensitivity and responsiveness on the part of the deputy minister. The regional development case, which is outlined later in this chapter, is an example of this type of agenda-setting.

Ministers who do not develop an agenda   In some instances ministers cannot develop an agenda because they don't know the policy field; the diversity of interests pressing the department precludes any definite course of action; or they prefer to respond to problems as they arise.

Ministers told us that about three-quarters of their colleagues develop some type of agenda within the first few months of their appointment. About 25 per cent never develop a clear agenda or set of priorities.

When this occurs, deputy ministers have problems. When ministers don't have an agenda, it is almost impossible to focus the energies of the minister, deputy minister, and chief political aide on a common purpose. If there is no agenda, the deputy minister has to manage the department without sufficient political direction and must respond to the minister's interest in various issues on an ad hoc basis. In this situation, deputy ministers frequently try to assist a minister to establish an agenda by using ministerial speeches and responses to particular issues to articulate a policy position or direction.

If the minister is unwilling or unable to set an agenda, the deputy minister has a hard time defining departmental priorities. Without some overall political direction it is difficult for deputy ministers to reconcile conflicting pressures from clients and central agencies. For this reason, the worst possible situation, from the point of view of deputy ministers, is a minister with no agenda.

One deputy minister explained the problem of supporting such a minister in the following words:

> *"I had major problems working effectively with my minister. I could not get a discussion with the minister about the overall agenda for the department. How could I carry out my accountability obligations to the minister without adequate communication and an unclear agenda?"*

Another deputy set out the opposite situation:

> *"The relationship between the department and the minister's office was absolutely superb, in fact, a model. The main reason for this is that the minister knew what he wanted to do and had a clear agenda. He selected his staff to achieve that agenda, and the political staff and department staff co-operated right from the start in achieving that agenda within their respective roles. What I think happens in many cases is that the minister has no agenda and there is a fight between the political staff and department staff about what the agenda should be."*

MINISTERS HAVE DIFFERENT APPROACHES TO AGENDA SETTING IN DIFFERENT DEPARTMENTS

Experienced ministers do not follow the same approach to agenda setting for every department to which they are appointed. Instead they adopt the approach best suited to a particular situation. For example, one minister took three distinct approaches to agenda-setting in three different portfolios.

In one portfolio this minister had a clear idea of his agenda before assuming responsibility for the department, as well as support in the form of government policy. In another portfolio he knew nothing about the department and there was little government policy or direction, leaving him more flexibility to develop his own direction. To do this he relied heavily on his political staff because he felt the department did not have the ability to develop the policy agenda he wanted. In a third department he carried on with the previously established commitment of the Government. Although he gave the necessary political direction to the department and carefully reviewed its work, he relied extensively on departmental officials to develop the required approach and provide the professional expertise.

4.3 THE ROLE OF DEPUTY MINISTERS IN SETTING THE MINISTER'S AGENDA

A major frustration faced by many ministers is that changes in policies and programs are difficult to accomplish. Not only is the central agency and collective management structure complex, but departments take time to change. Ministers need the support and co-operation of a skilled deputy minister to seek Cabinet approval for policy changes, obtain Treasury Board support for program and budget changes, and implement policy and program changes. As one minister said:

> *"It is very important for my agenda that deputy ministers know how the Cabinet and Treasury Board systems work and how to get things through the system. I would much rather see deputy ministers who know their way around the system than a bunch of Rambos wandering around."*

Consequently, ministers often judge deputy ministers on the contribution they make to defining, developing and implementing their agenda. This section describes how deputy ministers feel about this role and how they carry it out.

THE DEPUTY MINISTER'S PERSPECTIVE

It is of the utmost importance to deputy ministers that they develop a clear agenda with the minister and a clear understanding of their respective roles in implementing that agenda. They believe that these steps are critical to establishing an effective working relationship with the minister.

Deputy ministers use a wide variety of means to obtain information and direction about the agenda from the minister. Most develop a list of priorities that are discussed with the minister at departmental planning sessions. They arrange conversations with the minister on individual items or arrange to travel with the minister in order to secure a few hours of uninterrupted time.

They feel a deep obligation as professional public servants to ensure that management actions and policy development are consistent with the views and priorities of the minister. The ethic of a non-partisan public service that is committed to supporting the political priorities of ministers and the Government is very strong at the deputy minister level (see Chapter 6). This ethic is critical to ensuring that the public service is responsive to ministers. The absence of this ethic could require ministers to aggressively take control of departments, whereas its presence ensures that deputy ministers actively seek to be under political control.

Several deputy ministers said that they took satisfaction from being able to read their minister's mind or sense how he or she would react to an issue. To a considerable extent deputy ministers associate their success with the success of their minister. Finally, it was clear from our interviews that job satisfaction is greatest when a deputy minister helps a minister achieve a major policy or program change desired by the minister or the Government; this can seldom be accomplished without a clear agenda to establish direction and set priorities.

The views of deputy ministers about their role in agenda-setting are illustrated by these quotations.

> *"The minister had his political agenda based on his knowledge of the field and various agreements that had been established with provincial governments. His line was simple: `I have an agenda. It is the following....You manage the department, keep me out of trouble on department management and don't break any rules.' He assumed that I would read his priorities, know what he wanted, and support his agenda."*

> *"Agenda setting was simply a question of determining where the minister wanted to go and how we could help him get there."*

> *"The minister has to understand the department, have an agenda and do his homework. If he does these things, he will not have a problem with the responsiveness of the department or his political staff."*

> *"I believe in the need for a clear agenda. It is ideal. It works best when government and ministerial priorities are set along with department priorities. It is a mesh of all three. It seems to me that ideally there has to be a blending of all three of these together in terms of making sure that what is agreed upon can be effectively accomplished."*

> *"The minister had a clear idea of what he wanted to do in a couple of areas. After that the rest was up to me. I discussed with him the specific priorities that we had developed internally through our planning process. He added some of his own priorities and agreed to the overall plan."*

MANAGEMENT BY RADAR

To help ministers set and achieve their agenda in the context of the overall priorities and directions of the Government, deputy ministers scan their environment to understand the Government's and the minister's priorities and to identify the other factors that could influence their achievement. This could be called management by radar.

Deputy ministers send out signals to get readings from central agencies and others about the department. They read signals from the Government in the form of throne speeches, announcements by the Prime Minister or the progress of various items in Cabinet. They analyse and review speeches and statements by their minister and try to understand his or her priorities. In addition they work hard to understand the concerns of various groups that deal with the department, including parliamentary committees, interest groups, provincial governments, Crown corporations, and other federal departments and agencies.

"I try to set the agenda by anticipating the issues that I know we have some chance of managing. In terms of anticipating the issues, we monitor various situations and try to figure out what will emerge over the next few months. Where there are issues or areas you can control we have a systematic process in place and we move ahead. The ministers are involved in these areas and play an important role in endorsing the agenda and furthering it through their personal efforts."

"The fact that directions are not written on a piece of paper does not mean that I do not get signals. I can get them from speeches from the throne, budget speeches, central agencies, breakfast meetings."

Reading these signals and avoiding collisions is not easy. Conflicting signals from different sources require reconciliation. Deputy ministers should be adept at figuring out how to reconcile diverse views and interests. By interpreting the signals, deputy ministers try to assist the minister to develop an agenda that meets the needs of the minister and has the maximum possibility of success.

BALANCING THE MINISTER'S AGENDA WITH ESSENTIAL DEPARTMENTAL RESPONSIBILITIES

Although assessing and balancing external demands is essential, ministers and deputy ministers must ensure that the pursuit of key policy or program changes does not occur at the expense of the basic functions of the department (for example, protecting the health of Canadians, ensuring the safety of consumer products, safeguarding the viability of the fisheries). Even if the minister's attention is elsewhere, these primary ministerial responsibilities must be fulfilled.

When ministers stay in their departments for little more than a year or two (see Chapter 6) there is a strong incentive to focus on a few initiatives that will yield maximum political benefit rather than on the basic responsibilities of the department. If both ministers and deputy ministers change frequently, there is a danger that both will be preoccupied with achieving a particular short-term agenda and that little attention will be given to the department's basic operations.

One deputy minister noted that in his department successive ministers had quickly identified themselves with a few initiatives without concern for the basic role and functions of the department. Since most ministers in that department did not expect to remain there for more than a year, they felt that they had to accomplish something visible and noteworthy within that period. The deputy minister said that after a year in the portfolio ministers tended to become more concerned about the key functions and responsibilities of the department. He said:

> *"I had one minister for two years and it made a great difference. By the end of the first year he knew he would be around for a while. As a result, his behaviour in the second year was quite different. He started to look at how money could be used either for infrastructure or the future and how money could introduce change as opposed to dishing money out for events. It was then possible to get more mileage with these funds and to build an infrastructure with that money."*

Similarly, the deputy minister must guard against policy overload. One deputy minister had to advise a new minister that the previous minister had opened so many policy doors that the department simply could not afford to open another. The minister agreed and made his agenda one of consolidating the work of the previous minister. In this way, the deputy minister fulfilled his responsibility to manage the department in such a way that it would be able to support subsequent ministers as well as the current one.

An important facet of the deputy minister's job is thus to help the minister understand the critical functions of the department, ensure, on behalf of the minister, that these responsibilities are properly met, and involve the minister where necessary to seek direction on how these functions should be carried out.

WHOSE AGENDA IS IT?

Clearly, deputy ministers can play a major role in setting the minister's agenda. We asked ministers whether they felt co-opted into an agenda that was really not their own. None did.

When the ministers adopted an agenda proposed by the deputy minister, they felt completely responsible for it and viewed it as their own agenda, not that of the deputy minister. Even if deputy ministers propose agenda items, ministers know that deputy ministers are not responsible for setting the agenda. They said that deputy ministers usually propose items that reflect their minister's needs, personal interests or approach to the portfolio. Deputy ministers read speeches by the minister, enquire of other deputy ministers about the minister's interests in other portfolios, and review government and party policy before proposing initiatives. The following quotations illustrate these views.

> *"When I arrived, the DM said, `Your agenda is my agenda.' We never had any problems after that."*

> *"I gave my deputy minister a few ideas about what I wanted to do in a twenty-minute conversation. He came back to me in a few days with a document of several pages outlining a complete set of priorities and showed me exactly where my ideas fit within this overall plan. It was amazing to see how my ideas were reflected and captured into a coherent plan."*

Ministers know that because they can reject any proposal put forward by a deputy minister, they are ultimately responsible for agenda-setting.

4.4 IMPLEMENTING THE MINISTER'S AGENDA

Once the minister has established the agenda, the deputy minister has to work carefully with the concerned groups to establish support and secure resources and approval where necessary. A deputy minister's ability to stickhandle an issue through the maze of interests can be a precious asset for a minister. Effective deputy ministers are adept at managing in an uncertain environment and balancing conflicting goals, interests and perceptions.

To implement an agenda in the public administration environment, ministers and deputy ministers have to be able to process an enormous amount of information and make judgements about how it affects the minister's agenda. Most of the key information required comes from personal discussions, informal contacts and knowledge of the government system.[6] Ministers and deputy ministers seldom find that formal information systems, plans or guidelines provide sufficient information for them to make judgements about how to implement specific agenda items. Success depends to a large extent on the ability of the minister, deputy minister and chief political aide to co-operate in gathering relevant information and influencing individuals and institutions.[7] As one chief political aide said:

> *"To achieve the agenda of a minister, you've got to co-operate in working the networks. Ministers operate their network (e.g., Cabinet, caucus, interest groups),*

chiefs of staff operate their network (e.g., political advisers, Prime Minister's Office,) and the deputy ministers operate theirs (e.g., Treasury Board, Privy Council Office, department). In our department we work the networks individually, but with the same intent."

It is difficult for ministers to implement an agenda. It requires highly developed political and managerial skills to change a policy or program or to bring about new legislation.[8]

CASES: MANAGING THE AGENDA

The cases presented in this chapter illustrate the difficulty of managing an agenda, as well as the complexity and diversity of interests that must be dealt with and the multiple objectives that ministers must reconcile in order to pursue an initiative.[9]

The regional development case demonstrates how a minister reconciled an initiative with the overall government agenda and a variety of regional and economic interests and constituencies. Even though this policy initiative was consistent with the objectives of the Government, the minister and deputy minister faced a major problem balancing the minister's timetable for the issue with that of the Prime Minister and the Government. The issue was not considered to be one of the top two or three government agenda items, but it was of sufficient importance that it could have damaged the achievement of the Government's agenda in other areas. As a result, the minister's policy initiative had to gain the support of various players such as a Cabinet committee, the Department of Finance and the Privy Council Office at critical points in its evolution. When the minister was able to assure the Prime Minister and Cabinet that adequate consensus could be achieved on the issue, he was allowed to proceed.

In the mandate case the department was heavily dependent on the support of a variety of departments as well as the Prime Minister. Without a clear link between the minister's agenda and the Government's agenda it was unlikely that the change could have taken place.

The resource case contrasts very well with the regional development case and the mandate case. Unlike the regional development case, the lumber issue did not require major involvement or agreement from the Prime Minister, Cabinet or other agencies, remaining largely at the level of a ministerial agenda. However, a regional minister and Treasury Board had to be involved because of the potential resource implications. In addition, the minister faced a major challenge in obtaining the required support for the policy change among the client groups.

THE REGIONAL DEVELOPMENT CASE

A window of opportunity had opened to resolve a longstanding regional development problem. The issue was economically complex and politically sensitive. Any solution would be extremely expensive. The Minister had concerns about the problem as a result of his responsibilities in a previous portfolio. After discussing the matter with the Deputy Minister (DM), the Minister decided to make the issue his number one priority.

THE REGIONAL DEVELOPMENT PROBLEM

The essence of the problem was a longstanding constraint on industrial development in a region of Canada because of a deteriorating transportation system. A badly outdated agreement between the federal government and the transportation companies had established a fixed statutory rate for transportation of certain specified goods. In recent years, the transportation companies' profits had decreased significantly as inflation pushed equipment operating costs far out of balance with the fixed rate. Unable to raise rates or cut services, the companies reduced maintenance and shelved equipment acquisition plans.

The existence of the fixed rate had also created an obstacle for any industry producing goods that were not included in the fixed rate agreement. Over time, the availability of one method of transportation at artificially low rates had prevented development of other modes of moving goods. This situation, combined with the lack of expansion in the rate-bound transportation system, had created a bottleneck. Faced with an uncertain capacity to service markets, new industries could not grow.

The Department of Regional Development had been aware of these problems for years, but the groups enjoying the fixed rate were naturally reluctant to change the status quo, and they had strong political support for their cause. Recent studies had shown the groups, however, that failure to deal with the artificially low rate was resulting in millions of dollars in lost exports by hampering expansion in the transportation system. They warily began to suggest that changes to the rate regime might be considered.

The Government's political agenda at that time was almost totally occupied by two other policy issues of major significance, both affecting the same region as the transportation issue. The Minister and DM knew they would face opposition if they tried to introduce the transportation issue, owing to the risk of policy overload in the region. They were encouraged, however, by the knowledge that sufficient funds to address the problem could be available within the next year, through a special fund that had recently been established under Cabinet committee control.

SETTING THE MINISTER'S AGENDA

The Minister and DM both saw that action on the issue was necessary. They also agreed that even in the best of circumstances it would be very difficult to resolve this issue. However, they perceived that there was some possibility of successful action. Their shared view on the matter went beyond a pragmatic assessment of the environment. A personal chemistry and trust developed as they began to work together, based partly on personality and partly on the inherent challenge of resolving a very difficult issue.

Moving as a team, the Minister and DM visited provincial ministers and officials, key interest group leaders and other appropriate opinion leaders. In Ottawa, the Minister met with his colleagues and the DM met with other key DMs and central agency officials. So closely aligned was the understanding between the Minister and DM that if the need arose, they were able to carry on a subtle role-reversal, with the DM on the road, dealing with broad (though non-partisan) concepts and the Minister in Ottawa, handling issues that might otherwise never have reached his desk. This partnership produced a momentum that would carry the policy through difficult times. The DM was also able to mobilize a very competent team from the Department to assist him on the issue.

MOBILIZING SUPPORT

While the DM found broad support among departments and central agency officials based on the increased economic efficiency that would result from implementation of the proposal, the Minister was faced with persuading his colleagues that change was necessary and practical. It also became clear that he would encounter stiff competition for the funds needed to ensure the viability of his initiative.

At the end of the first year, the issue was put on the shelf by the Prime Minister, citing "not enough consensus on the issue". Undaunted, the Minister and DM reinforced their position with firm cost data, detailed design of a consensus process, and mobilization of supporters in the private sector. After two years of negotiation and consensus building, government support in principle, including funding, was secured.

An innovative consultation exercise followed, led by a relatively unknown but competent and politically astute individual appointed by the Minister from the non-government sector. Through four months of intensive negotiations with the many interests involved, a formula for solving the problem was produced.

A task force was formed, in which the DM was an active and regular participant, to draft the required legislation. During this period, it became clear that a final hurdle needed to be cleared. A strong regional lobby was demanding changes to key financial provisions in the legislation. The DM met with the regional caucus several times, presenting a blitz of facts and data supporting their plan. Concurrently, the Minister sought to alter caucus opinion through personal persuasion. Their efforts met with only limited success.

CHANGED LEGISLATION

The final hurdle was crossed when the Minister and Prime Minister agreed to change the disputed provisions in the legislation. This secured the support of caucus and the regional interest groups.

OBSERVATIONS

The case illustrates how with a clear shared agenda and good working relationship a minister and deputy minister can tackle major problems involving complex and conflicting interests. The flexibility, degree of openness, and trust in the working relationship enabled the Minister and DM to support each other and to adapt to new events and problems. During the entire process it was clear to the Minister that he was accountable to the Prime Minister and to Parliament. It was also clear to both the Minister and the DM that the Minister was publicly responsible for the success or failure of this initiative and that the DM's role was to support and advise the Minister. The DM was also conscious, however, that the success or failure and, more generally, the manner in which the issue was handled would affect his own future standing.

THE MANDATE CASE

The Department of Defence Production (DDP) had been established in the 1950s to co-ordinate the full range of activities associated with acquisition of defence equipment, including requirement definition, R&D, contracting, regional economic issues and foreign trade. During the 1970s, the influence of the Department had diminished as other departments had successfully exerted greater control over their respective areas of expertise. By 1976, DDP had lost its departmental status and had become a small agency reporting to the Minister of National Defence.

By 1982, it was not clear that the Defence Production Organization, as it was now called, would continue to exist at all. It had been criticized for years as being ineffective, and many central agency officials and ministers had wanted to abolish it. This ineffectiveness had been caused in part by a lack of influence — since its co-ordinating function lacked any program or regulatory operations — and in part by high turnover of senior officials. During a recent election campaign, however, the Prime Minister had given considerable emphasis to revitalization of the Armed Forces, particularly on the acquisition of badly needed replacements for the aging land, sea and air fleets. When forming his new Cabinet, the new Prime Minister appointed a Minister of State for Defence Production (MSDP), signalling that a decision had been taken to do something further with the organization.

MSDP was the first Cabinet appointment for the new Minister. When he took office, the Minister moved boldly to develop his own plan for the ministry. His plan took the form of proposed organizational changes, including the acquisition of some line departments' defence equipment contracting operations. This was a striking departure from the organization's traditional co-ordinating role and would clearly be seen as an unprecedented takeover. A new deputy minister was appointed three months after the Minister arrived. He had extensive experience in managing defence acquisition programs at the senior ADM level and knew well the dilemmas faced by the new ministry and its previous history of ineffectiveness.

The DM was a strong supporter of an enhanced role for MSDP, but he found two major hurdles in assisting the Minister with his agenda. First, the Minister was inherently suspicious of the public service. Second, the DM knew that the Minister would run into serious interdepartmental roadblocks if the DM did not assist him to develop a more pragmatic version of his proposals and establish the necessary prime ministerial support to overcome departmental reservations. The DM clearly understood that the Minister was accountable to the PM for the success of the ministry. The DM's role was to provide the Minister with the best possible assessment of the situation and to take subsequent action in accordance with the Minister's decision. The twofold challenge for the DM would be to advise the Minister to modify his approach while assuring him that he was not trying to derail the Minister's agenda in favour of his own.

In concert with his Minister, the DM focused on securing a precise mandate letter from the Prime Minister to the Minister. The letter would provide an essential point of departure for changes to the role of the ministry. He was able to take advantage of three circumstances to aid his cause. First, there was the pro-defence climate that had resulted from the Government's election platform and recent Throne Speech. Second was the work of a recent expenditure task force, headed by a senior minister, which had uncovered several problems relating to co-ordination of defence spending with the government's regional development goals. Third was the revelation by the Minister of Finance that the government's promises of expanded defence spending would have to be cut back in the context of a larger than expected deficit. The result of these three factors was that the Privy Council Office and the Prime Minister's Office were looking for some agency to handle the policy and program co-ordination issues that would soon emerge.

Taking advantage of this top-down pressure as well as the bottom-up lobbying by MSDP, a mandate letter was obtained from the Prime Minister that reflected a set of roles, powers and tasks that the Minister and his DM regarded as basic to enhancing the stature of the ministry and to building greater confidence in its role among key players in the federal policy process. The letter was distributed to all ministers that would be affected by the Prime Minister's instructions to the Minister of State for Defence Production.

Over the next several months, the Minister and DM cultivated the new mandate. The DM devised a workplan to carry out the mandate and to ensure that no slippage resulted from the counter-pressure of agencies long critical of the ministry's record. The Minister and DM placed particular emphasis on obtaining the personal support of the senior Minister who had headed the expenditure task force.

The Minister was moved to a more senior appointment after only 18 months with the ministry. The new Minister was sent a mandate letter that was essentially the same as the one obtained by his predecessor. With the aid of his DM, he continued the process of establishing a role for MSDP that was understood and supported by other departments and agencies. Within a year, MSDP was given resources to double its staff. Several MSDP Cabinet submissions were approved over the same period, providing the Minister and DM with confidence in the strength of the ministry's new mandate.

OBSERVATIONS

This case illustrates how issues can move from a minister's agenda to the Government agenda and the importance this can have for a small department that requires the co-operation of Cabinet and other departments to make a change. The mandate letter to the Minister from the Prime Minister provided an essential point of departure for the Minister and Deputy Minister in developing and enhancing the role of the organization. The letter also clarified and confirmed this change in the role of the ministry as a government priority. This helped achieve the necessary co-operation of other ministers and departments to strengthen the ministry's new role.

THE RESOURCE CASE

A newly appointed minister of the Department of Resource Development (DRD) was confronted with a problem in the lumber industry that had been described by some as nearing crisis proportions in one region of the country. Production overcapacity, depressed markets, increasing costs and dwindling resources had been identified in a major government study. An interdepartmental task force had made hundreds of recommendations for change that would affect the industry in one region of the country.

THE RESOURCE PROBLEM

The Minister recognized the lumber issue as one of his top three priorities, but he knew that he would have little time to deal with it. His personal attention was more urgently required in two other areas of current concern to the Government - an urgent resource management policy issue and a serious federal-provincial jurisdictional conflict.

The interests concerned with management of the resource were divided into several broad categories, with many specialized interest groups. The interested parties included the pulp and paper industry, a variety of producer groups and associations, recreational users of forest lands, and financial backers. Although they all agreed with the need to solve the resource management problem, agreement soon dissolved when discussion turned to decisions on specific means. Nonetheless, any policy that did not achieve broad consensus among these diverse interest groups was not likely to succeed.

WORKING OUT THE ROLE OF THE POLITICAL ADVISER AND DEPUTY MINISTER

The Deputy Minister (DM), also new to the job, had little experience with resource management problems in that particular region. The Assistant Deputy Minister (ADM) responsible for the region could offer only limited assistance. Existing policy was dated and the Department did not have sufficient expertise to deal with the complexity that would be inherent in a new policy. In addition, officials were fully occupied with implementing the Minister's two other priorities.

Although preoccupied by his other two priorities, the Minister remained concerned about the lumber issue. He was aware that the problem had been treated by a band-aid approach in the past and he was not convinced that the Department planned a more comprehensive solution this time around. To safeguard his interests, he turned the issue over to his long-time chief political adviser. He gave the adviser virtually complete authority to speak on his behalf.

Within a few months, the Minister's adviser had become involved nearly full time on the issue, holding discussions and even negotiations in the region with the industry and associated interest groups, including other ministers and MPs. Since the adviser believed that the departmental staff immediately responsible for developing the policy were unwilling and probably incapable of responding to the Minister's wishes, the ADM responsible for the region and, to a lesser extent, the regional director general were excluded from the initial phase of this policy development exercise.

DEVELOPING POLICY IN A CONFUSED ACCOUNTABILITY STRUCTURE

The Minister and the DM, meanwhile, had taken action to improve the Department's policy development capability. Through discussions with the

Secretary to the Cabinet, it was decided to appoint a Senior Assistant Deputy Minister (Sr. ADM) with the general mandate of strengthening policy development and the immediate task of handling the lumber issue. The Sr. ADM and the Minister's adviser were able to work, if not closely, at least co-operatively on the policy. The Minister was very pleased by the policy support of the Sr. ADM. While this was a positive development for progress towards a workable solution, the DM, who was pressing forward on the Minister's other two priority issues, became further distanced from the lumber issue.

Over the next six months, the four-way accountability relationship that had formed at the apex of the policy decision process introduced further confusion into an environment that was already plagued by disagreement among the major players on both substantive and tactical issues. These disagreements extended to differences between officials in the region and headquarters on the approach to resolving the problem. Officials wanted a simple but coherent package that approached the problem from the perspective of the Department's traditional mandate and that made incremental changes that could be supported by the interest groups. The Minister and his adviser pressed for what they saw as a complex but more realistic policy that took a broader view of the department's resource management role and that called for fundamental changes in the resource management regime.

A policy was finally developed that met the needs of the Minister, but it did not achieve support among the interest groups involved. The policy was rejected by the interest groups, leaving the lumber issue unresolved. The exercise was nevertheless deemed a political success by the Minister and by an influential regional minister, since a policy had been developed and publicly announced where one had not previously existed.

In any case, economic conditions had improved in the last few months and the demand for action had receded. The Minister was further encouraged, because his other two top priority issues had been successfully implemented.

OBSERVATIONS

The case illustrates some of the difficulties when a minister is faced with one more agenda item than he can reasonably handle. Because the Minister had two other major agenda items and the Department was not responding quickly enough to the long-standing problem, he relied heavily on his special assistant to carry out his ministerial responsibilities and publicly stated that his assistant spoke on his behalf. This created a complex and difficult working relationship between the Minister, DM, and other players.

Although the Sr. ADM was formally responsible to the DM for developing a policy, the existence of two mandated extra players (the Sr. ADM and the political adviser), with whom the minister dealt directly on the issue, introduced confusion and complexity into the normal accountability relationship between the minister, the

DM and the Department. This arrangement ultimately produced a policy, but it became very difficult to establish a clear agenda among the four major players which, in turn, made it more difficult to achieve the necessary co-operation and consensus with interest groups.

4.5 FINDINGS: MANAGING THE MINISTER'S AGENDA

In the 150 instances of agenda-setting covered by our interviews, most ministers felt that deputy ministers were responsive to their priorities and accountable for their performance. There was strong consensus among ministers, regardless of the governments in which they had served, that in the final analysis they chose their own agenda and were responsible for the priorities set for the department. In almost all cases, ministers viewed the deputy minister as a key contributor.

Co-operation between ministers and their deputy ministers is critical to effective agenda-setting. Ministers and deputy ministers share the narrow neck of an hourglass. Both are subject to competing pressures that complicate the process of establishing and implementing an agenda.

The research shows that if a minister is to implement an agenda successfully while simultaneously carrying out the basic responsibilities of a department, there must be excellent teamwork between the minister and deputy minister based on a good understanding of their respective roles and abilities.[10] For deputy ministers, it is essential to establish some agreement with the minister on the agenda if they are to carry out their management functions. With a clear ministerial agenda, a deputy minister can communicate the minister's priorities to the department and provide leadership in the midst of conflicting demands. As most experienced and successful ministers indicate, both the deputy minister and the minister gain by setting a common agenda and by trusting and supporting each other.

Conversely, if the minister and deputy minister are unable to establish a clear agenda and agree on how they will work together to achieve it, there is little chance that they will be able to accomplish anything significant. This is illustrated by the resource case, where strained relationships among the major players made it much more difficult to achieve the minister's agenda.

In summary, deputy ministers face the following challenges in developing and implementing a minister's agenda:

—— ascertaining the minister's agenda or priorities and achieving the co-operation and trust of the minister and chief political aide;

—— reconciling the minister's priorities with conflicting demands and pressures from outside groups or central agencies;

—— responding quickly to ministerial priorities in large, complex departments facing numerous financial, organizational and administrative constraints; and

—— balancing the short-term aims of the minister with the longer-term need for stability and political commitment to the basic functions and management requirements of the department.

The research shows that the problem the federal government faces in the area of agenda-setting is not the accountability or responsiveness of deputy ministers to the political priorities of their ministers. The problem is how to ensure that minister-deputy minister teams have the experience, knowledge, and complementary skills to develop and implement an agenda, and the means and environment necessary to achieve the minister's and the government's objectives. These are among the issues explored in the remaining chapters of this report.

CHAPTER 5 MANAGING THE DEPARTMENT

T hus far in this report we have dealt primarily with the problems faced by ministers and deputy ministers in dealing with each other, with their colleagues, and with the many external forces that they must reconcile. In this chapter we turn our attention inward, to the departments they manage.

Departments are the implementation arm of the government. Ultimately, it is the public servants within departments who deliver the Government's programs and implement its policies. Consequently, ministers must be sure that their departments will be responsive to their direction and that they will operate within the collective management practices established by Treasury Board and other central agencies.

It is the job of the deputy minister to harness the capabilities of the department and manage it on behalf of the minister. By managing, we mean the entire range of activities associated with directing a large and diverse organization within a complex environment. Depending on the department and circumstances, this normally includes some combination of activities such as budgeting, organizing and planning, and activities such as negotiating, motivating, communicating and influencing. Deputy ministers are expected to know the mind of the minister well enough to manage the department as an informed extension of the minister. The value that they should add to the minister's direction is threefold: knowledge of the department; familiarity with the requirements of collective management; and the objectivity of a non-partisan perspective.

The chapter begins with an examination of the challenges faced by deputy ministers when initially taking charge of a department. The following section explores the problems deputy ministers must overcome to make the department capable of responding to the minister and, equally important, willing to be responsive. These leadership tasks shed light on the areas of department management that deputy ministers consider to be the most critical. The chapter concludes by examining the accountability system of private sector chief executive officers to determine whether private sector experience can be applied to solving some of the problems in the public sector.

5.1   TAKING CHARGE OF A DEPARTMENT

Modern federal departments are complex organizations encompassing an extraordinary variety of activities. Departments range in size from fewer than 400 employees (Privy Council Office) to more than 120,000 (Department of National Defence). The geographic distribution of employees varies, from the highly centralized Treasury Board Secretariat to the highly decentralized Department of External Affairs. Complicating the physical dispersion of personnel is the diversity of employees found in most departments. The Department of National Defence, for example, has over 63 different classifications of civilian employee groups in its establishment, ranging from PhDs in physics to accountants to public relations officers.

Taking charge of such organizations and making them respond to ministerial direction is a daunting management task. The quotations on the following page illustrate the kinds of management challenges that deputy ministers may encounter. In considering the difficulty of dealing with such challenges, it is useful to remember that the career path that leads to becoming a deputy minister is not necessarily one that provides a great deal of management experience. Many of the deputy ministers we interviewed had spent nearly their entire careers in policy positions. This gave them good experience in working with a broad, government-wide perspective, but provided little experience in departmental operations.[1]

When asked about their priorities in taking over a department, deputy ministers invariably mentioned the importance of learning about the department; scanning the environment for high-risk areas; ensuring that adequate management and information systems were in place for finance, personnel, security, and so on; and establishing sound processes for planning and control of departmental policies, programs and operations. These steps provide a foundation upon which the deputy minister's management of the department can be built.

THE CHALLENGE OF DEPARTMENT MANAGEMENT

"The most significant challenge I faced was getting articulated in some form what the department was all about, and trying to accomplish this in a way that could be supported 100% by my minister, and then communicate this adequately all through the department to provide motivation to the employees."

"A big challenge for me was relations with the industry. The industry is angry in good times and in bad times. I concluded that the choice was dissipated discontent or concentrated fury. I always tried to control this towards dissipated discontent."

"For me, it was very important two months after I arrived, that we provide a framework for this large organization. We needed a system that would improve communications, improve results in operations, and remove subjectivity. I wanted to create a spirit among all the people who work here, that they work for a fantastically good cause."

"I soon realized that the branches of the department are really independent management organizations in their own right. A group of feudal dukedoms. They each contain all the administrative machinery within the branch. It's not easy to get a handle on what is going on. The corporate group had functional elements, but they were always trying to find out what was going on in the branches."

"A major challenge was to co-ordinate the development of policies by the department with development and implementation of policies by agencies, such as Crown corporations or regulatory agencies, who operate at arm's length. You have to achieve a degree of co-operation because the public doesn't understand that the left hand doesn't necessarily know what the right hand is doing"

"When I arrived there were hostile clients, a hostile press, and a hostile Auditor General. There was a strong group arguing that the department was not spending enough money and just as strong a group arguing that there was too much money being spent. In addition, there were many random events that constantly destabilized the department. There were many management changes required. On top of all this, we had a suspicious minister and a suspicious minister's office."

LEARNING ABOUT THE DEPARTMENT

Most deputy ministers are appointed to departments where they have had no previous experience. At the time this report was written, more than 75% of deputy ministers headed departments where they had not previously had any experience. It is not suprising, therefore, that most deputy ministers emphasized the enormous challenge of initially learning about the responsibilities of a department. They pointed out that effective management calls for personal knowledge of the structure, capabilities, role, and culture of the department and an equally good knowledge of external forces, such as clients and interest groups. Even if this information is readily available from subordinates and departmental files, absorbing it is time-consuming.

The initial months in a new portfolio are a busy time for deputy ministers, as they must begin to introduce themselves into the activities of the department while trying not to slow operations. Concurrently, they are getting to know the minister, and establishing themselves with internal staff and external contacts. Even experienced deputy ministers find this period difficult. Inexperienced deputy ministers are particularly hard-pressed to carry out these initial tasks quickly enough to take charge effectively in the short term.

> *"The most difficult thing for me was to try and bring myself up to date on the working of the department while at the same time meeting the day-to-day needs of the minister. Here I was trying to learn the ropes of being a deputy minister, trying to be briefed about the department, while the minister was trying to move ahead and to establish new directions and initiatives. In that kind of situation deputy ministers always feel somewhat uncomfortable, because you are bare: trying to organize for the minister, trying to make sure he gets the best of advice, thoughtful advice, but you feel that you cannot contribute a great deal, because you don't have the knowledge."*

Deputy ministers must act quickly and wisely to reduce the vulnerability created by their lack of knowledge of the department. They do not feel that they can serve the minister well without personal knowledge of nearly all aspects of the portfolio.

Some examples illustrate the variety of fundamental, department-specific factors that must be mastered by a newly appointed deputy minister.

Client/Interest Groups   Nearly every department has client or interest groups that must be dealt with by the deputy minister. For the most part, these groups are unique to each department. There are few similarities, from the deputy minister's perspective, between the clients of Agriculture Canada, for instance, and the clients of Fisheries and Oceans, even though both deal with resource issues. Consumer and Corporate Affairs and Environment Canada both have regulatory functions, but the politics, tactics and personalities involved in the lobby groups for each department are quite distinct. Deputy ministers must become familiar with the politics, the players, the issues, and the strategies of these client/interest groups if they are to manage the department effectively.

Nature of Expenditures   All departments spend money, but the nature of expenditures can vary widely, and with it, the nature of the deputy minister's involvement in the expenditure management process. For example, the budget of the Secretary of State is not large, but includes nearly 6,000 grants to non-government organizations. Each grant must be considered individually and in many cases must be given final approval by the minister. The sensitivity of these grant programs means that the deputy minister must often become involved in decisions concerning relatively small amounts of money. In contrast, the deputy minister's involvement would be low where there is a high proportion of non-discretionary, statutory expenditures, such as Health and Welfare.

Diversity of Department Programs   Deputy ministers were keenly aware of the need to find a way to handle the variety of issues that cross their desk within days of being appointed:

"An important challenge was the diversity of the subject matter. We deal with vastly different subject areas involving research, regulation, technology, and social and cultural issues. Also there is extreme diversity of activities. You have to deal with downsizing, disciplining an employee and a problem in technology, then launching a new program and then an international agreement."

Policy/Operations Orientation   Deputy ministers pointed out that there is great diversity among departments with respect to the proportion of policy activity to operational activity. Policy activity involves formulating options for government action on current issues, drafting legislation, and similar functions. Operational activity encompasses a broad spectrum of functions, ranging from processing income tax returns to food inspection.

Figure 5-1 illustrates the range of policy/operations diversity of departments in the federal government.[2] The Department of Finance, for example, is a small department that deals almost exclusively with high-profile policies. It would thus be in quadrant 4. Revenue Canada is a larger department that is largely involved in operational activity alone, and would therefore be in quadrant 1.

The location of most departments is likely to change over time, especially along the policy activity axis. Nevertheless, the interviews confirmed that the management requirements of departments vary from one location on the chart to another. There are certain useful similarities between, say, National Defence and Transport Canada, but the difference between managing Public Works and managing External Affairs is significant.

FIGURE 5-1

DEPARTMENT MANAGEMENT REQUIREMENTS

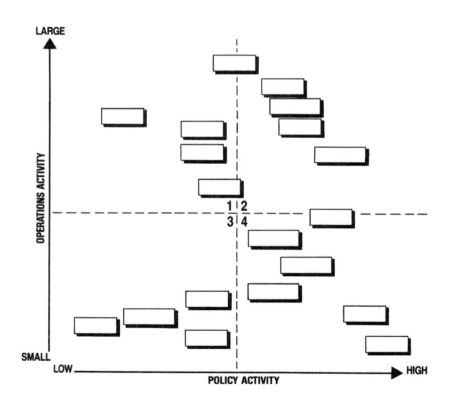

SCANNING THE ENVIRONMENT FOR
HIGH-RISK ISSUES

Deputy ministers know that in the highly complex and diversified environment of most departments, they always run a risk of being caught unawares by an issue. In the first few months, their lack of knowledge about issues or operations increases that risk. To protect the minister and the department from damage caused by a foreseeable incident, most deputy ministers carry out an early assessment of the internal and external environments to determine where the greatest risks lie.

In one case, a deputy minister described the importance of assessing risk and taking action to reduce it. This deputy minister had recently been appointed to a department that delivered a variety of social programs. Many of the programs were implemented through locally appointed, not-for-profit service agencies. Although the minister was ultimately responsible to Parliament for the work of the agencies, the agencies tended to be independent and resisted direction from the department.

Early in her tenure, the deputy minister realized that improper administration by any of these agencies could cause injury to the clients of the department and might embarrass the minister and the Government. She resolved to keep a close watch for problems.

Within a few months, the deputy minister's assessment proved correct. Symptoms of trouble, in the form of anonymous letters and rumours accusing one particular agency of poor administration, reached her office. She dispatched officials to investigate the agency and found several serious irregularities in operation and administration of the agency. A series of meetings with agency directors followed. Corrective action was promised, but it never materialized. A few weeks later, after consulting the minister, the deputy minister obtained authority to fire the local management team and have the department take over the agency temporarily. By recognizing this potentially hazardous situation early in her tenure the deputy minister was able to defuse it before a serious incident occurred.

Scanning the environment for potential problems is an ongoing task for deputy ministers. In the enforcement case, the deputy minister becomes aware of an issue that is not on the minister's agenda but could become a problem in the future. The challenge for the deputy minister is to persuade the minister to take prompt action on the issue despite significant political constraints.

MANAGEMENT AND CONTROL SYSTEMS

Deputy ministers cannot manage the complex operations of their departments properly without sophisticated management and control systems. A high-profile administrative blunder can weaken a minister's credibility enough to jeopardize his ability to move the department's programs through Cabinet. Failure to deliver a promised program may destroy a minister's confidence in a deputy minister. The following paragraphs describe the involvement of deputy ministers in two major areas of management systems and controls: those that seek to ensure compliance with administrative regulations, and those that involve planning and implementing departmental programs.

Administrative Controls When we asked deputy ministers to talk about the challenges of managing their departments, they seldom spoke of problems with functional areas such as financial administration, personnel administration or security. In most cases, controls and systems for handling day-to-day administration were in place and were working to the satisfaction of the deputy minister. In some cases, new systems were being developed on the direction of the deputy minister, but this was less common.

Two factors act to reduce the amount of time deputy ministers spend on ensuring administrative regularity. One is the low risk associated with delegating these tasks; the second is the minimal relevance of these activities to the day-to-day needs of the minister.

If there is any part of the deputy minister's role that approaches a quantifiable task, it is in the area of financial, personnel and other administrative duties. In contrast to the highly subjective roles of policy advice and executive management, the technical requirements of expenditure control, staffing, security, and information management are well documented. Countless pages in departmental and central agency manuals are devoted to documenting the machinery in place to support these functions. Deputy ministers can delegate with confidence in these areas to specialized departmental staff. Further, the regular audit, evaluation or review of departmental activities by both internal and external agencies helps ensure the regularity and efficiency of operations.

Deputy ministers are aware, nonetheless, of the possibility of being blindsided by a random event such as an administrative blunder or an intentionally dishonest act. Even a well managed department can be plunged into a front page scandal overnight. Such incidents cause embarrassment for the minister and, in extreme cases, result in calls for the minister's resignation. The amount of time the deputy minister

THE ENFORCEMENT CASE

The Deputy Minister (DM) of a department dealing with law enforcement had proposed a policy to his Minister that would focus needed enforcement effort on a growing area of illegal activity. The Minister recognized the value of the proposal, but both he and the Department were currently under political attack for being insensitive and unreasonable with the public on another enforcement issue. He could ill afford to announce a tough new enforcement policy.

The DM had visited the offices of similar enforcement agencies in other countries. While the incidence of illegal activity was higher in those countries than in Canada, he was struck by the sophistication of their enforcement operations. He became convinced that with illegal activity on the rise in Canada, the Department needed to adopt some new measures.

From the DM's managerial perspective, the optimal policy would be closely linked with an effort to invigorate the Department's morale and sense of mission. His senior officials were fully supportive. There had been discussions under previous DMs about new approaches to enforcement, but they had not resulted in new enforcement initiatives.

The Minister-DM relationship in the Department was characterized by a lack of in-depth ministerial involvement in department management. This was in part because of the complexity of the laws and regulations administered by the Department and in part the normally low-profile nature of the policies involved. Ministers were rotated through the Department on a frequent basis and generally did not have time to become familiar with the often arcane details of field operations. Ministers provided broad policy guidelines, then relied on DMs to devise detailed policies within these boundaries and to manage the Department.

The Minister was in a very uncomfortable position to be announcing a new enforcement policy. He had been facing an almost daily onslaught of questions in the House of Commons and in committee regarding the allegedly heavy-handed implementation of the Department's enforcement policies. The mere mention of new enforcement initiatives would prolong opposition and media preoccupation with the current issue.

The DM recognized that this was a difficult time to propose new enforcement initiatives to the Minister. However, he also realized that the enforcement problem was serious and that it could lead to problems for the Minister or for future ministers if concerted action were not taken soon. The DM decided to advocate the change largely to improve the effectiveness of the Department in accomplishing its mandate.

When the DM raised the enforcement problem, the Minister was supportive, but he preferred that the DM devise a way to proceed that would satisfy both the Minister's current problems and the Department's longer-term concerns. After extensive consultation with departmental experts, the DM selected an enforcement plan that would strengthen enforcement measures where the chance of illegal activity was judged greatest, while reducing regulation of legitimate public activity. The Minister gave his support to the DM's plan, provided that the Department proceeded within his guidelines, particularly with respect to any dealings with the public.

The DM had determined that the entire initiative could be carried out within the statutory jurisdiction and budgetary resources of the Department. With this flexibility, he proceeded with detailed planning without consulting central agencies. He consulted other line departments whose co-operation he needed, but the Privy Council Office and Treasury Board were not formally involved.

Within a month of receiving the Minister's approval, the DM appointed a Task Force to develop and implement the new program. Inside the Department, the project involved a mobilization of resources that produced an immediate and contagious sense of mission among those involved. The goals of the program were simple, clear, and directly related to the Department's mandate. This generated enthusiasm even in those not directly associated with the initiative.

The program produced immediate and dramatic results. The number of successful enforcement actions increased significantly, while interference with activities of the general public actually decreased. When these numbers began to appear, the Department opened communication lines with the media. The program was hailed as a considerable success, bringing credit to the Minister and the Government. In subsequent months, the Government became more concerned about the enforcement problem and was able to launch a major policy initiative, based partly on the enforcement program that the Department had put in place.

OBSERVATIONS

The new enforcement program was initiated by the Department based on the experience of officials and on information taken from the enforcement environment. The DM put the program forward for the Minister's consideration, despite less than optimal political conditions, because he saw it as a necessary evolution of the department's role and as a necessary initiative to fulfil the Department's responsibilities for enforcement. The Minister was able to look beyond the current political turmoil to approve implementation of the enforcement program, subject to his conditions.

The case illustrates how a Minister and DM can successfully develop a common agenda that meets the current concerns and needs of the Minister and the longer-term needs of the Department.

The advantages of a good working relationship between the Minister and DM are also demonstrated. The DM's relationship with the Minister permitted him to raise the enforcement issue in difficult circumstances. Similarly, the Minister would not have approved proceeding with such a sensitive issue without complete trust in the DM.

must then spend to deal with the problem is often far out of proportion to the actual seriousness of the incident. Vulnerability to the random event is considered to be part of the job. When such events occur, damage is minimized by taking quick remedial action, assessing the system to determine whether repetition can be prevented, and improving safeguards if necessary.

The second major disincentive to spending time on matters of administration is that in terms of the minister's information needs, the deputy minister's detailed involvement with procedures and systems does not pay high dividends. In departments with a high level of policy activity, time spent by deputy ministers on administrative matters may not provide nearly the payoff to the department that time spent on policy can do. Most deputy ministers recognize this and use their time accordingly.

Program Management Deputy ministers must ensure that the department can produce desired operational results (i.e., taxes are collected, fish stocks are protected, pension cheques are distributed, etc.). Over the past 10 years, initiatives by the Treasury Board, the Office of the Comptroller General, and departments themselves have resulted in installation of comprehensive planning and control systems in nearly all departments. The systems provide a means by which deputy ministers may hold their departments accountable to them for results.

Most deputy ministers use one or more components of a corporate planning and control process. The process usually involves a structured collection of department-wide systems and processes designed to co-ordinate, control, and evaluate the department's plans, budgets, and operating procedures. Some of the stated aims of the process are to define the accountability framework within which departmental operations will be conducted; to ensure that priorities and other goals become the focus of attention in operational planning; to provide a mechanism for comparing plans with results; and to link operational planning with strategic planning.[3]

Such processes are particularly suited to departments with a high proportion of operational activity, because their relatively stable operating environment permits the deputy minister to delegate operations to senior managers within an agreed plan and leave them to manage. In fact, some variation of this process is virtually essential for these departments if the deputy minister is not to be overwhelmed by department activities. As one deputy minister said:

> *"You must understand the extent to which things are decentralized in this department. There are a lot of decisions here that I don't participate in. The place is so big."*

In recent years departments have supplemented their planning processes with annual retreats. At these one- or two-day meetings, top management, including the minister, deputy minister and assistant deputy ministers, discuss the coming year and set priorities.

Some deputy ministers' corporate management processes include formal managerial contracts. These deputy ministers feel that such contracts are an essential accountability tool. One deputy minister described how the contracts operate:

> *"The operational plan is decoded and translated into management contracts that I sign with each one of my executives in the organization. I revise the contract quarterly, if there are deviations, and to do that I set in place a functional control authority. I use functional heads to advise me on a quarterly basis whether they feel that in the light of the contract there has been any deviation, and if so, why. Their appraisal is based more on reality, it is less subjective, and is based on results achieved."*

Another means of refining the corporate management process is issue management. This practice is necessary in environments that require frequent guidance and communication from the deputy minister or minister, such as the department of the Secretary of State or Finance.

The corporate management process and its refinements underscore two facts about accountability within departments. First, deputy ministers are very aware that to get results they must provide their senior managers with mutually understood expectations. Second, accountability takes a different form below the level of deputy minister. In contrast to their own complex, often intangible system of accountability, many deputy ministers work to make the accountability system for assistant deputy ministers and other officials as quantifiable and consistent as possible.

In summary, deputy ministers must ensure that systems to control administrative practices and to promote sound program mangement are in place in the department. Once these systems are in place, deputy ministers can delegate responsibility for running them and free their time for managing the less controllable aspects of their environment.

5.2   THE LEADERSHIP CHALLENGE

While deputy ministers agreed that they could not manage their departments without formal management systems and controls, they clearly considered that systems provide only the basic tools for managing a department. In order to provide the minister with a truly responsive department, they must provide motivation to departmental staff and secure their commitment.[4]

The box on the following page shows one deputy minister's view of the executive functions of a deputy minister.[5] It is not the role of administrator. Deputy ministers have to be leaders, team builders, decision makers, and communicators to provide the necessary direction to a department.

THE NEED FOR LEADERSHIP

Recent literature in the private sector suggests that the increasingly complex management environment has created a greater need for leaders at every level of organizations.[6] The challenges of increased global competition, reducing costs, increasing productivity, and improving customer service have forced businesses to take a hard look at the leadership skills of their managers. A similar emphasis on the value of these skills has recently emerged in the Canadian public service. Downsizing, technological change, greater demand for services, and changes in program and policy orientation have all contributed to a need for more and better leadership in the public sector.

The nature of government often creates management challenges that are unique to the public sector. Deputy ministers often mention the problem of maintaining morale and motivation in the presence of public sector constraints and the uncertainty of the political environment. For example, they regularly emphasize the need for probity, prudence, and excellence in all facets of departmental work. They see this as particularly important when making recommendations, such as selection of contractors, that are highly visible to public scrutiny. When political considerations override such departmental recommendations, it may be difficult to convince staff to put their best effort into the next recommendation they make.

Problems of this nature are not solved by planning, directing and controlling. Most deputy ministers believe that managing in the traditional sense is not enough. As one deputy minister said in a recent speech:

THE EXECUTIVE FUNCTIONS OF THE DEPUTY MINISTER

CORE COMMUNICATIONS CHANNEL

"The deputy minister is the fundamental communication channel between all elements within the organization and among the department, the minister and outside agencies or groups such as central agencies, provinces, etc. There is no substitute. If you are the core communication channel you have to be stable."

DECISION MAKER

"Because the deputy minister has more information than anyone else, he or she is the main decision maker on recommendations to the minister."

LEADER AND MANAGER OF THE SENIOR EXECUTIVE TEAM AND STAFF

"A deputy minister has to develop a management team. The ADM's job is to work with the clients, who are extremely demanding and who demand a lot of time. As head of the department family, I have a responsibility to my department and staff. The deputy minister has to be careful not to be a bottleneck. Therefore, delegation is required. If there is delegation from the central agencies to the deputy minister, but there is a bottleneck at the deputy minister level, you have not gained anything."

MANAGER OF THE ENVIRONMENT

"You cannot control the environment because when heads of agencies or Crown corporation don't like something, they so to the minister. The same is true of the Clerk of the Privy Council, who interacts directly with ministers at Cabinet. So it is very difficult to deal with all of these relationships. You have to influence them, work with them, and co-operate with them."

"Management experts tell you to plan, organize, staff, direct, budget and control with insight and finesse and if you do, you will get positive management results. But without motivating your staff, you simply have technical management." [7]

Deputy ministers respond to this leadership challenge by building a competent, reliable management team and by sensitizing the team members to the minister's interests and priorities. They then focus on managing the external environment, so that the team can carry on with their work, and on communicating organizational goals throughout the department. They intervene when necessary to manage specific issues and make specific, politically sensitive decisions.

BUILDING THE MANAGEMENT TEAM

Deputy ministers cannot implement the minister's agenda without the aid of their senior officials. Even deputy ministers who are intimately familiar with their departments are precluded by time pressures from participating in the detailed aspects of policy formulation or program management. Deputy ministers must therefore build a team capable of carrying out the minister's agenda with the minimal direction permitted by the deputy minister's and the minister's schedule.

The constant organizing and re-organizing of government attests to the problem of dividing the many diverse areas of government activity among a relatively few departments. Inevitably, disparate activities will end up in one department. Consequently, it may be a major challenge to create a co-operative attitude among senior officials. The mere fact of being gathered under the same roof is not sufficient reason for groups with diverse technical or program objectives to operate as a cohesive department.[8]

The authority to deliver services, funds or even policies is often dispersed within a department so that each departmental group must depend on other groups to assist or support its programs. As the various groups interact, they find that the diversity of their clientele, objectives, and time horizons creates resource and policy disputes. These disputes become more acute in times of downsizing, sometimes requiring intervention by the deputy minister. In the department downsizing case, the deputy minister used a potentially divisive staff reduction to actually strengthen the department management team and to help the organization focus on its key priorities.

One recurring consequence of diversity in departmental activity is what deputy ministers call balkanization:

"In the several years before my appointment as deputy minister, there had been about 8 deputy ministers and about 11 ministers in the department. When I arrived, the department was a very diverse and heterogenous group that was not well integrated. I wanted to establish a sense of continuity and a management team. I think that my being there as long as I was (several years) helped me to be able to turn the department from a series of Balkan-like states into a more cohesive whole."

The fact that so many deputy ministers mentioned the problem of balkanization indicates that it is seldom solved permanently. For one department, we were able to interview most of those who had been deputy minister over the past 15 years. All, including the current deputy minister, had encountered the balkanization problem, and most had attempted to resolve it in some fashion.

The most common method cited by deputy ministers for promoting cohesion within a department was use of committees and department-wide planning processes:

"How do we keep a degree of coherence and cohesion? In our department, I use a second-in-command, the senior management committee, and the strategic planning process."

Deputy ministers recognize that the responsiveness of a department to clients and to the minister is often directly related to the deputy minister's ability to manage intradepartmental conflict. Left to themselves, departmental groups may deal with conflict by simply ignoring each other and finding solutions, albeit less effective ones, on their own.

SENSITIZING THE DEPARTMENT TO THE MINISTER

Once a management team is in place, it must be given the means to operate effectively with minimal guidance. Many deputy ministers found that this was best achieved by giving the team direct exposure to the minister. Needless to say, this is a tall order for any deputy minister. The research indicates that deputy ministers themselves may see the minister for less than 3 hours each week.

The promotion from assistant deputy minister or associate deputy minister to deputy minister was described by deputy ministers as a quantum leap. One deputy minister, who had full confidence in the functional abilities of his assistant deputy ministers, was nonetheless "constantly amazed at the political naivete evident in the proposals they bring to me". The most striking difference between a deputy minister and officials at lower levels appears to be the deputy minister's unbuffered exposure to the political environment of the minister. Even after an entire career spent working for or around politicians, newly appointed deputy ministers are often shocked by the reality of being the first level of contact with the minister.

Deputy ministers must bridge this gap in political sensitivity. They must make senior officials aware of the minister's and the government's political objectives and constraints so that they can take account of these factors in their work. Reliance on stated objectives and principles, however, will provide only an approximation of the minister's intentions. Further, the department is likely to face many decisions on items that are unusual or beyond the scope of written objectives. To be most effective, the management team must be given a good sense of the minister's personality, including background, interests, and method of approaching a problem.

Deputy ministers use two particularly effective means to facilitate this sensitization process. The first is to create, with the co-operation of the minister, a departmental round table, including the deputy minister, the minister, the chief of staff, political staff, and several senior officials.[9] The group meets regularly to discuss progress on major issues, with all those in attendance participating and benefiting from ministerial guidance and group synergy. The value of having the officials exposed to the minister's thinking process was noted by a minister's chief political aide:

> *"We have a unique forum in our round table meetings. The meetings are particularly useful because they let the officials see where the Minister is coming from in a broad sense. They can then better guess what his position might be on specific issues."*

The round table method is well suited for departments working on several aspects of a large issue, where all the officials around the table are working on closely related topics. A second method is often employed in departments with greater diversity of activities, where the wider variety of issues reduces the value of having the minister participate directly in intradepartmental discussions. In these departments, deputy ministers often allow assistant deputy ministers or other senior officials to brief the minister personally, usually in the presence of the deputy minister. The deputy minister advises the minister based on the content of the briefing. Again, officials have the opportunity to observe the minister's thinking process for future reference.

Whether group or individual meetings with the minister are held, a necessary condition for success is that the deputy minister must allow officials to speak their mind to the minister. A deputy minister who lacked confidence or jealously guarded his influence with the minister

THE DEPARTMENT DOWNSIZING CASE

OVERVIEW

The Department in this case was small and highly decentralized, and it was regarded as a junior portfolio for ministers. In recent years, the Department had been a frequent target of restraint programs, despite its growing activities and demands from client groups for implementation of recently updated legislation administered by the Department. The legislation changes alone would nearly double the Department's client load. The Deputy Minister (DM) was sure that if the Government failed to respond to these demands in a timely fashion, clients would take this as a strong signal that the Government's commitment to them was wavering.

Nonetheless, one month after appointment, the DM received a letter from the Secretary of the Treasury Board stating that another round of downsizing had arrived. The DM would have to manage the expanding operations while reducing person years by 1.5% annually for the next three years. In addition, the Department would have to find resources for policies or programs required from within existing allocations.

To further complicate the problem, time to develop a plan was limited. The Department's Multi-Year Operational Plan (MYOP) update was due at Treasury Board in four months. A staff reduction plan would have to be completed and approved by the Minister for inclusion in the update.

MANAGING THE DOWNSIZING EXERCISE

The DM saw the downsizing as an opportunity for corporate bridge-building within the Department. Although the DM and senior assistant deputy minister (ADM) were certain they could identify areas for reductions without extensive consultation, the DM decided that it would be beneficial for the branches to decide jointly on their reductions. The primary role of the DM would be to shape the internal management system by determining the process to be followed in formulating the staff reduction plan. The DM then delegated the actual plan formulation to a two-tier committee system comprising all the Department's senior managers. Over a two month period, the lower tier would examine options, alternatives and consequences and would present a final report to the senior committee. This committee, chaired by the DM, would determine which options to present to the Minister.

Over the next several months, the downsizing exercise occupied more 25% of the DM's time. In addition to meeting with the departmental review committees, the DM attended a series of meetings with the Deputy

Secretary of Treasury Board, with public service union representatives, and with the Minister or his staff. These formal processes were augmented by frequent informal contacts at all levels.

The DM also had to contend with eight study teams that were analysing the Department as part of a government-wide program review. While these teams were not directly involved in the downsizing process, the DM had to manage the interface between the teams and the Department in order to minimize interference with the essential task of planning the staff reduction.

The Minister was not extensively involved in the process, since most of the downsizing options involved internal policy, services, communications and administration. The DM ensured that managers were sensitive to the political realities of their proposed reductions, however, and the Minister's staff were kept informed.

At the end of the decision-making process, the DM met with the Minister to present and discuss recommendations. The DM advised the Minister regarding the potential impact of the reductions on service to the public, internal administrative and communications support, flexibility and timeliness in providing policy support on major issues, and workforce readjustment problems. The DM also expressed the view to the Minister that the reductions would jeopardize the Department's ability to fulfill its mandate, particularly with respect to the Government's recent commitments to the Department's clients.

The Minister made the final decisions regarding which programs or services could be cut, necessitating some re-working of the options that had been prepared by the Department. On the Minister's direction, the DM included the staff reductions in the Department's next MYOP update and carried on with implementation of the reduction plan.

OBSERVATIONS

The case illustrates how the DM must manage the Department to accomplish both short-term goals (meeting the downsizing target) and longer-term objectives (creating an effective management team and implementing legislation) while dealing with the demands of a diverse set of responsibilities to ministers, central agencies, unions, staff, clients, and others.

Even though the Minister did not choose to become directly involved in the downsizing exercise until late in the process, the DM was clearly accountable to the Minister for the management and results of the downsizing effort. When presented with the Department's recommendations, the Minister played an important role in deciding on the areas where the reductions would be made.

might not be able to cope with the loss of power implied by having officials carry issues to the minister. Even a strong deputy minister would want to ensure that the minister understood the rationale for presenting issues in this manner so as not to jeopardize the minister-deputy minister link. One deputy minister related the initial problems the minister had with this method:

> *"One of my practices was from time to time to have a breakfast meeting with the minister with my assistant deputy ministers present. I did not consider myself a funnel or filter, so they could speak to him about their issues and I would comment if necessary. One minister, who was perhaps expecting a different style, could not at first understand why I was putting all of the issues on the table for discussion with him in an open forum with my subordinates. It took him a while to understand that I was not abdicating my role — it was just my style."*

In departments where the minister-deputy minister relationship is strong and working well, the minister and his staff understand the deputy minister's motives in strengthening the management team in this way. A chief political aide told us that:

> *"It is just not possible for the deputy minister or even his ADMs to know all aspects of issues. Both the minister and I realize this and we do not consider that the deputy minister is weak or ineffective if he lets his staff explain an issue."*

Deputy ministers found that sensitizing senior officials in this way paid exceptional dividends. The deputy minister's ability to delegate is enhanced by the knowledge that officials are not working on the basis of politically naive assumptions. In addition, exposing senior managers to the political process is a valuable training and development opportunity.

COMMUNICATING GOALS THROUGHOUT THE DEPARTMENT

The importance of communicating departmental goals to all levels of the organization was emphasized by ministers, deputy ministers, and assistant deputy ministers. Without the co-operation of all employees, especially those involved in implementation, little can be accomplished; explaining decisions to employees in terms of rational goals is an essential part of securing that co-operation. One assistant deputy minister in a large operational department explained it this way:

> *"We have to get to the people who are running the front end of our operations and explain why we are doing things. This is especially important when we make changes. We must convince them that there are good reasons for the changes."*

Getting the minister's direction through to front-line employees is a common concern. Ministers are not always convinced that senior departmental managers can diffuse ministerial directions down through the bureaucracy to a level where clients can see results. This is especially true in departments with an identifiable client base, such as fishermen, farmers, senior citizens, veterans, or the unemployed. Ministers normally feel a strong sense of personal responsibility to these clients and are frustrated if they cannot quickly and effectively change the way the department treats these clients. One chief political aide voiced this concern:

> *"I don't believe that any official was trying to actively subvert the minister's aims, but I was frustrated by seeing the translation from what the minister wanted to what the clerk in B.C. was telling the public."*

Deputy ministers have a major role to play in communicating corporate goals and specific ministerial direction. They must gather information from a variety of sources within the department and from the external environment and disseminate this information to employees in such a way as to move the organization in the desired direction. The content of their communication may be factual, such as interpretation of central agency directives, or value-oriented.[10] One deputy minister explained how he went about communicating corporate goals and values to employees:

> *"The health of the organization is as good as the front line is perceived. If even one individual doesn't understand what we are trying to accomplish, you can miss out. Three months after I arrived, I imitated how the private sector were involving their people. I developed a mission statement to confirm what business we were in. I then articulated that statement in an operational way, so that people could develop a sense of where they were going, what they were doing on a day-to-day basis, and what that meant to our customers."*

Many of those interviewed were concerned, however, that the most basic messages, such as "Improve Service to the Public" or "Be More Accessible to Clients", were not getting through to front-line employees. Similarly, the concerns of front-line staff, including feedback from clients, were not reaching senior management. Somewhere along the network, communication is breaking down.

A recent study of managerial attitudes in the public and private sectors provides evidence that the communication breakdown is occurring at middle management levels.[11] The study found that a dramatic reduction in satisfaction with the organization and loyalty to the deputy minister occurred as one moved down the public service hierarchy. The authors observe that middle managers belong to a "separate management culture" from senior managers, with different perceptions and assessments of the management environment.

Three factors may contribute to this breakdown. The first is the sheer size of departments and the many levels in the hierarchy. In large departments, it is not unusual to find middle managers with no idea who the deputy minister is, how he thinks, or what he is trying to accomplish. This is in sharp contrast to the private sector, where CEOs of large corporations told us that they make sure staff know who they are and what their goals are. The anonymity of public servants prevents deputy ministers from using high-profile communication strategies. This factor, combined with the size of departments and the turnover of deputy ministers, tends to isolate middle managers from the thinking of senior managers.

The second factor is the tendency of individuals in a complex environment to focus on the goals of their own unit rather than the goals of the overall organization.[12] Regional offices can be particularly susceptible to this tendency when they are confronted with local problems daily and only an occasional memo or directive to let them know head office exists. To overcome this tendency, senior managers must constantly restate the goals of the organization to all personnel in a clear, consistent way. Deputy ministers cannot carry out this vital role if they stay only a short time in a department, and many deputy ministers feel that if they do not do it, it will not be done. As one deputy minister told us:

> *"The most important thing, which nobody else will deal with if I don't, is the behavioural pattern of the employees. In a broad sense, the leadership of personnel is one of the most important things that I do."*

The third factor that may interfere with effective communication is the inclination of those acting in a professional capacity to feel accountable to the values of their profession. These values may sometimes compete with the values or goals of the organization. In the past, the definition of a professional was restricted to members of legally constituted professions, such as engineering, law, and medicine. In recent years, the definition has been broadened to include a high level of occupational expertise.[13] Thus, we have professional researchers, professional purchasing agents, and a wide variety of others, who may feel that the ethics of their profession are of at least the same importance as the values or even the direction of senior managers. One deputy minister described how the orientation of his department towards the values of its primary profession had eroded the ability of staff to respond to political considerations, such as regional concerns, in making their recommendations. He had to convince them of the requirement to weigh these concerns in order to make realistic recommendations to the minister:

> *"I had to manage the culture of the department to make it more sensitive to the priorities and agenda of the minister. My problem as deputy minister was to get the department to understand the importance of serving the minister well, and that the minister has a right to be served."*

Deputy ministers and assistant deputy ministers are responding to the communication challenge by emphasizing departmental goals at meetings, seminars, and planning forums for managers. One assistant deputy minister we interviewed was using video tapes of the Throne Speech and of the minister and deputy minister describing how they wanted the department to respond to the speech. He presented the video tapes, followed by a question-and-answer session with his managers. Another assistant deputy minister takes every possible opportunity to attend seminars involving his personnel and talks about what he is trying to accomplish.

The challenge of communicating corporate goals is an essential feature of managing departments; it requires constant attention to ensure that the department remains responsive to the minister's needs. It is not clear, however, that deputy ministers are winning this battle. This has serious implications for the responsiveness of departments to ministers and deputy ministers.

5.3   THE CHANGING MANAGEMENT NEEDS OF A DEPARTMENT

We questioned deputy ministers about their previous departments as well as their current responsibilities. We were able to get a perspective on the management requirements of several departments over time. This perspective was enhanced by interviews with retired ministers and deputy ministers.

One observation that emerged is that the management needs of a department can change over time and even overnight. This has serious implications for the deputy minister. Can a deputy minister who has been focusing his attention on operational matters suddenly undertake the responsibilities of being chief spokesman to the media concerning an intricate international legal problem? Can an expert on high-profile policy-making guide a department successfully into the implementation phase?

There are several distinct phases through which departments can pass, some transient, others medium to long-term.

High-Profile Policy   This situation is characterized by the presence of one or more policy issues of national importance that require extensive time and effort to manage. The deputy minister must provide policy advice to the minister and help him or her work with central agencies, other departments, provincial governments, and the media. Day-to-day management of the department must be delegated. The regional development case (Chapter 4) is an excellent example of a department in this phase.

Turnaround   Departments in this situation have suffered a serious setback in the recent past, in the form of a financial fiasco, public outrage, or similar event. The Government has usually been embarrassed, and the public may have lost some degree of confidence in the department, or at least in its management. Revenue Canada (Taxation), the Department of Regional Industrial Expansion, and the Canadian Security and Intelligence Service have gone through such periods in the past 10 years. The deputy minister's job is to turn the fortunes of the department around. The deputy minister's attention is concurrently downward and outward. The twofold problem inside the department is to provide whatever is necessary to resolve the problem that precipitated the damaging incident, and to repair damage done to departmental morale and self-image. The deputy minister must help the minister convince the public that the problem is resolved or is being resolved. The minister and deputy minister must agree on the pace of the turnaround. The minister may be under public pressure for a quick turnaround. The deputy minister must assess the ability of the department to withstand change at this pace and must advise the minister accordingly.

Operations   This is the "business as usual" condition for most departments. Policies and programs are being proposed, approved and implemented, but there is little going on that is on the Government's primary agenda. The Department of National Defence and Customs and Excise may normally be characterized as being in this phase. However, the character of these departments can change, as happened with National Defence with release of the recent White Paper on Defence. The main activity of the deputy minister in the operations phase is to keep the department running smoothly, making efficiency improvements where possible. A deputy minister whose department was in this operational mode said:

> *"I have never had the sense that anybody was interested in or cared what we do, as long as we stay out of trouble and we don't get involved in juicy little scandals. Most ministers who come to the department operate on the same agenda, and there are not a lot of high-profile or partisan issues."*

The leadership challenge for the deputy minister is to keep department morale high while dealing with basic operational functions. The deputy minister should advise the minister that change is not required at this time; this may be difficult if the minister is looking for an agenda that will raise his political profile. On the other hand, the deputy minister must get the attention of central agencies and Cabinet on issues which the department wishes to move forward, even though they are not high-profile.

New Direction   This situation occurs when a department embarks on a change of direction of sufficient magnitude to change the way the department carries out its mandate. In an extreme case, the mandate itself may be changed. A deputy minister who was managing a department in this phase made these comments:

> *"This is the year of the greatest policy change in the history of the department. It is the end of economic regulation. It is the end of infrastructure building. It is a very fundamental change."*

The job of the deputy minister shifts towards management skills, because the change may involve significant reduction or addition of personnel, centralization or decentralization of operations, and modification or implementation of planning and information systems. Some emphasis will be placed on consulting external agencies and clients about the new direction, negotiating new relationships, and obtaining approvals where required. The mandate case (Chapter 3) is an example of the management requirements facing the deputy minister in this situation.

Revitalization   This situation is perhaps the most difficult to identify, especially from outside the organization. A department in this circumstance has become run down and is in need of rebuilding. The symptoms may range from morale problems to financial administration difficulties. The problems are not severe enough to be noticed by most external agencies, but there is no doubt to the astute observer within the department that responsiveness and effectiveness are at a low ebb. One deputy minister described such conditions:

> *"The problems I faced in assuming responsibility for the department were a policy shambles—which is basically, if it growls feed it with money; overhanging agreements and unresolved negotiations; problems with impact of changes in other federal programs; a demoralized organization; a bad financial information system; and major problems and conflicts with clients."*

Frequent minister and deputy minister turnover can lead to this condition. The challenge for the (usually new) deputy minister is to identify the lacklustre portions of the department and to provide the leadership necessary to rebuild them. This can be even more difficult than the turnaround phase, because there is not always a specific problem that can be isolated and solved.

In summary, deputy ministers must always ensure that the most current assessment of the department's situation is used when making departmental plans. They must recognize that a different leadership approach may be called for in new circumstances and that they must adapt accordingly.

5.4   ACCOUNTABILITY IN THE PRIVATE SECTOR

Frequently, politicians, public service managers, and analysts of the public sector reach into the private sector to find solutions to the problems of managing government. The purpose of this section is to explore the validity of this approach.

We interviewed 21 chief executive officers (CEOs) in Canadian companies about accountability in the private sector. We asked CEOs about the accountability relationships in their companies. To whom and for what did they feel accountable? How did they deal with the multiple demands of their board of directors, shareholders, customers, regulatory bodies, and employees?

There are some areas, such as human resource management, where useful parallels may be drawn. However, a blanket application of private sector management solutions presupposes that there are uniformly similar conditions in both sectors. One of these conditions of similarity should be the practice of accountability. In the interviews the CEOs had clear and consistent views on the subject of their accountability, enabling us to make a useful comparison with the accountability system of deputy ministers. The evidence shows that despite some similarities, the nature and mechanisms of accountability are fundamentally different in the private sector.

Analysts in both the public and the private sector have for years made lists of sectoral comparisons.[14] Some have carried their analysis to the deputy minister/CEO level, coming to the not unexpected conclusion that there are both similarities and differences in the jobs. When we interviewed CEOs and deputy ministers who had held CEO positions, they spoke more often of the vast differences than of the similarities. CEOs were uniformly astounded at the deputy minister's management environment as depicted in the agenda-setting chart (Figure 4-2) and the management environment chart (Figure 2-1). As one CEO observed, "I'd need a psychiatrist if I had to work in that environment."

This reaction was usually combined with expressions of respect for the quality of the senior public servants who manage in what most CEOs consider a very difficult setting:

> *"I have been very impressed by the public servants that I have met. I sympathize a lot with the difficulties of their role in serving ministers and dealing with the political process."*

THE BOARD OF DIRECTORS

Knowledge of the business is held in very high regard in the private sector. The premium placed on such knowledge is reflected in the composition of most boards of directors. In the companies we sampled, it was not unusual to have board members with 15 years on the board and even longer experience in the industry. Companies often maintained continuity by moving retiring CEOs to the position of chairman of the board.

The implications of this depth of knowledge for the accountability of the CEO are significant. First, the CEO can draw on a wealth of company-specific knowledge when seeking advice on strategy or tactics. Even if the experience of some directors is dated, the CEO can apply the lessons learned to present-day problems. Second, the CEO knows that the expectations about his performance will be adjusted relative to the performance of the economy or at least the industry as a whole. The CEO will not have to explain in detail why a predicted return on investment was not achieved when the entire industry has fallen short on this performance indicator. Third, and most important, a board is consistent in its goals and direction over time. CEOs can make long-range plans with confidence and can weather short-term lows with greater ease because of this long-term perspective. As one CEO noted:

> *"Certainly I'd have a problem if the Board directed me to do something that I considered to be dangerous for the company, but the point is, they just wouldn't do it. They know better than that."*

ACCOUNTABILITY OF THE CEO

The management environment of a CEO is often extremely complex. Rapid technological change, the problems associated with entering international markets, and other factors present CEOs with difficult challenges. CEOs told us, however, that clear understanding of their roles and responsibilities and those of the people to whom they are accountable enables them to manage the complexity. They were able to maintain a stable centre in the midst of their environment. This clear and stable accountability relationship does not guarantee that a CEO will be successful, but CEOs felt that it permits them to approach their jobs with a confidence and directness that may not be possible for deputy ministers.

Most CEOs spoke about their accountability with confidence and precision.[15] They were clear about their degree of freedom and the limits on their actions and could predict the likely outcome of both good and poor performance on their part. Three characteristics of their accountability regime were frequently mentioned: the single-line nature of CEO accountability; the mutual agreement on specific, often quantifiable performance expectations; and the latitude given the CEO to achieve results.

Single-Line Accountability Most CEOs quickly and clearly identified the one person or group to whom they are accountable. This is normally the board of directors. In companies with majority shareholders, primary accountability was to this shareholder, through the board:

> *"I am accountable to the Board of Directors and my company is accountable to me. I must deal with the demands of clients, suppliers, market analysts, etc., but they are not in the direct line of accountability."*

> *"I am hired and fired by the majority shareholder. He holds the most seats on the board and uses the board as a means of holding me accountable."*

> *"I am accountable to the Chairman of the Board, who owns all of the shares of the company. We have a Board of Directors, but it only exists to fulfil the requirements of legislation."*

CEOs commented frequently with respect to the multiple accountability of deputy ministers. They believed that it would be extremely difficult for any person or group to hold the deputy minister accountable or for deputy ministers to manage their departments effectively. As one CEO noted:

> *"The deputy minister's environment looks like a matrix organization that I worked in once. It was very difficult to get true accountability because when you would ask someone to do something they could say `But that diverts me from this other task that I have'."*

The accountability of CEOs is exercised both formally and informally. In companies where the board holds real power over the CEO, formal meetings of the full board may be held monthly or quarterly. Where boards meet less than quarterly, meetings of committees of the board, such as the audit committee and executive committee, are held with the CEO on a more frequent basis. Informal meetings of the CEO and individual members of the board are common, allowing the CEO to address the individual concerns of board members and increasing time available at full board meetings for discussion of broader issues.

In some cases, accountability was to a majority shareholder or a head office:

"I meet with the majority shareholder once or twice a year for a couple of hours to discuss plans for development and diversification of the company. I take the overall business plan to the Board once a year for ratification. The Chairman usually makes the approval decision without much input from the Board."

"I have a boss in head office in the United States. We speak on a weekly basis on operations and monthly I send him the financial statements. He has just this week reviewed my proposed budget for next year. He didn't like the profit figures so I have to do some more work on that. We will eventually present the plan to the U.S. Board, but there is no doubt in my mind who hires and fires me."

The Performance Contract CEO accountability is normally linked to a specific, mutually developed and agreed upon budget or plan. The components of the plan range from specific financial goals (e.g., 18% return on investment over the next 12-month period) to detailed personnel development objectives. Seemingly soft objectives, such as involvement in community projects or charitable causes, are often quantified, as in "charitable contributions will be 1% of annual profits", and are factored into the agreed upon bottom line. The plan is presented by the CEO at a board meeting. Board members nearly always receive meeting material ahead of time and prepare questions. The plan is debated and either approved or returned to the CEO for amendment. Once approved, the budget or plan becomes a working document for which the CEO feels totally accountable. CEOs consider the annual budget or plan an accountability contract with their board. We asked CEOs how they would feel if the board directed them to deviate from the plan. One CEO expressed what was a common view:

"I would definitely feel less accountable if I had to follow instructions from the Board of Directors that negatively affected the objectives that we had agreed upon. This would be a constraint."

Management Flexibility Within the boundaries of an annual plan and any mutually agreed financial or other broad-based limitations, the power of the CEO to manage is considered to be nearly absolute. CEOs said that their ability to manage human resources by hiring or moving people around in the organization is the most valuable area of flexibility. Any constraint on this freedom would be a serious blow to their ability to achieve results.

Another type of flexibility often mentioned by CEOs was their ability to make most decisions away from public scrutiny.

"I have recently felt some of the media problems that must be encountered regularly by deputy ministers. An aspect of one of our aquisitions caught the media's attention and I now have to deal with the fact that every decision I make could be in the paper tomorrow. I couldn't operate like that on a daily basis."

Market analysts and the business press may be quick to comment on the more visible activities of corporations, but most CEOs feel that they can manage in relative privacy. They consider the fishbowl environment of the deputy minister to be a management liability.

5.5 FINDINGS: DEPARTMENT MANAGEMENT

The ability of a deputy minister to make the department responsive to the minister is crucial. Highly developed policy and negotiation skills and familiarity with the government environment are necessary attributes for deputy ministers, but they are not enough. The deputy minister must be able bring the department's resources to bear on the minister's agenda items and on other matters within the department's responsibility. Without active involvement and direction by the deputy minister, the department may be pulled away from the minister's needs by the many strong external forces in its environment.

Comprehensive systems for planning and control of departmental activities and expenditures are essential tools for deputy ministers. These systems help ensure probity, prudence, and regularity in departmental operations and permit evaluation of program results. Deputy ministers cannot rely on systems, however, to help them balance the competing demands of the minister, the department, and the external environment. Systems do not build teams, elicit co-operation or motivate personnel. To achieve these goals, which are essential to make effective use of the department's capabilities, deputy ministers must exercise leadership skills and sound judgement based on a combination of abilities, experience, and knowledge of the department.

Several factors, including the profile of policy issues, political scandals, and high turnover of management, contribute to change in the management needs of a department. These changes can occur overnight or over several years. As management needs change, so does the mix of skills, experience and knowledge required in the deputy minister. The success of deputy ministers as department managers depends on whether they can meet the needs of the department in its current circumstances. This condition must be a consideration in selecting or moving deputy ministers.

The research on accountability in the private sector makes it clear that deputy ministers cannot be considered the CEOs of their departments. Most CEOs are able to rationalize competing external demands in terms of their accountability to a board of directors, or at least to a major shareholder. In contrast, deputy ministers must measure their actions in terms of four different (and sometimes mutually exclusive) accountability demands.

Ministers may appear to carry out some functions of a board of directors, but their decision-making horizon is far shorter, their understanding of the department's business is often restricted to a few current issues, and they rarely have the same trust relationship with the deputy minister that a CEO has with a board. In addition, ministers must work within the volatile priority environment of government and must direct their deputy ministers accordingly, often changing priorities overnight.

The net result of these differences is that deputy ministers cannot manage their departments as CEOs manage their companies. They are held accountable by their ministers for an entirely different range of expectations than are CEOs. Their freedom to exercise management prerogatives that CEOs consider essential, such as hiring practices and resource management, is constrained by accountability for achieving collective management goals. Notwithstanding these differences, there must be an ongoing examination of private sector management practices by those within government, with the view to finding and transferring those practices that may be usefully applied to public sector problems.

From the point of view of deputy ministers, it is becoming more and more difficult to manage departments. In the past several years, federal departments have become increasingly complex through the development of new programs and functions. In addition, deputy ministers face considerable challenges with respect to downsizing and communicating priorities to their departments, while at the same time responding to new ministerial initiatives and the continuing needs of clients.

While departmental management is placing greater requirements on deputy ministers, their time is increasingly occupied with other tasks. As we mentioned in previous chapters, deputy ministers have to spend more time playing a broker role between ministers and ministers of state; co-ordinating with the minister's office; and responding to parliamentary committees on behalf of the minister. It is therefore becoming more difficult for deputy ministers to balance the need to provide direction and management leadership to departments with the demands of their other functions.

6 **MANAGING THE DEPUTY MINISTER GROUP**

Throughout this report I have tried to show why it is such an enormous leap of faith for ministers to trust their deputy ministers with such vital tasks as formulating policy options, representing them to clients and the media, and managing their departments. Not only must they trust the loyalty of their deputy ministers, they must also trust that they are competent to carry out these tasks. This chapter examines the question of whether ministers are being provided with a sound foundation on which to base this trust. Are they getting the best possible deputy ministers?

The starting point is an analysis of the deputy minister tenure problem mentioned in earlier chapters. Nearly all deputy ministers told us that the brief duration of deputy minister appointments is a problem, and they encouraged us to develop statistics on the subject. To understand the benefits that can derive from longer tenure, we look at the career patterns and tenure of chief executive officers.

A formal process exists for assessing the competence and overall performance of deputy ministers. We review this process and present the views of deputy ministers regarding its accuracy, fairness, and limitations. We also look beyond formal systems to a more fundamental question — is there a public service ethic upon which ministers can depend for the loyalty of their deputy ministers? Finally, we take a brief look at how ADMs feel about becoming the deputy ministers of the future.

6.1 JUST PASSING THROUGH: TENURE OF DEPUTY MINISTERS

One persistent notion about deputy ministers is that they are like the old bass lurking at the bottom of a fishing hole. They remain in departments for years, even decades, ruling their domain as they wish and using their vast and detailed knowledge of the department to control the endless parade of ministers.

An examination of the time in office of deputy ministers totally refutes the notion of long tenure. Over the past two to three decades, deputy ministers have spent progressively less time in their posts. Correspondingly, the average duration of a minister-deputy minister team has also decreased. Ministers, deputy ministers, parliamentarians, and ministerial staff expressed concern about the duration of appointments and its implications for performance and accountability.

THE STATISTICS

The statistical population included all deputy ministers and ministers, from departments, ministries of state and central agencies, who were in office between January 1, 1960 and December 31, 1987. The population included 434 ministers, 227 deputy ministers, and 605 minister-deputy minister teams.[1] The box on the following page provides examples of the findings. The following paragraphs cover some of the specific research questions.

How long do deputy ministers remain with departments?   The early 1960s marked the end of an era when deputy ministers stayed with their departments for very long periods. There are some extreme examples, such as Health and Welfare and Revenue Canada/Customs and Excise, where deputy ministers had started in the 1940s and had remained for nearly 20 years.

In the late 1960s and early 1970s, the practice of rotating deputy ministers began in earnest. Figure 6-1 illustrates the effect of this practice on the deputy minister population. Average tenure has been declining since the 1960s. In 1966, it was 4.5 years. In 1976 it was 2.1 years. In 1987 it was 2 years.

Figure 6-2 shows the number of deputy ministers between 1960 and 1987 whose appointment lasted three years or longer. The period of three years was chosen because in the view of many deputy ministers it represents the amount of time required for a deputy minister to become fully effective.

Only rarely since 1969 has the number of deputy ministers with three or more years in a department exceeded 40 per cent of the deputy minister population. The valleys in Figures 6-1 and 6-2 are caused in most cases by elections, followed by major deputy minister shuffles. At one point, following the election of 1974, only 6.5 per cent of deputy ministers had been three or more years in their departments. While

SOME STATISTICS ON DM TENURE

— In 1987, the average DM had been in his or her current department for 2 years

— In 1987, 50% of DMs had been in their current department for less than 1.5 years

— 9 Departments had 3 or more DMs during the period 1984-1987

— The average duration of a minister-deputy minister team during the period 1984-1987 was less than 1 year

FIGURE 6-1

AVERAGE DM TENURE
1960-1987

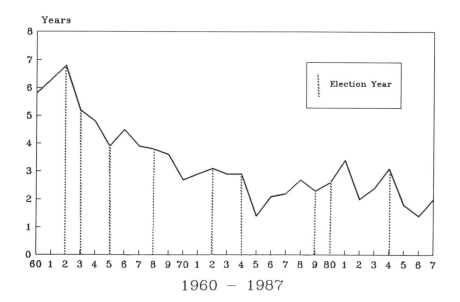

1960 — 1987

FIGURE 6-2

DEPUTY MINISTERS
More than 3 years with Dept.

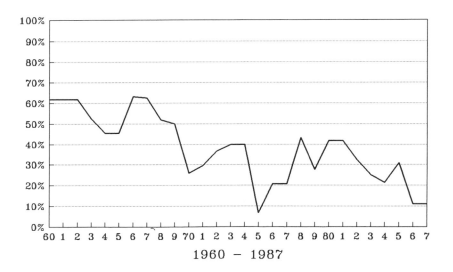

1960 – 1987

there is a rebuilding of deputy minister tenure after each valley, the subsequent peaks have been getting lower for at least the past ten years.

How much total experience as deputy ministers do deputy ministers have? Five years seems to be the minimum time required to produce an experienced deputy minister who could be considered a true corporate resource. The deputy minister would probably have had at least two portfolios during that five years.

Not unexpectedly, the more experienced deputy ministers are more confident in their ability to handle their duties. These deputy ministers generally have a better understanding of the machinery of government, have worked with more ministers, and feel more comfortable with the ambiguity of the environment. It is clearly an advantage to the government to have a cadre of trusted, experienced deputy ministers available for reassignment to difficult portfolios. Somewhere between the battle-scarred and weary 20-year veteran and the inexperienced novice should be a seasoned professional who would be valued by nearly any minister as an adviser and by younger deputy ministers as a mentor.

Figure 6-3 illustrates the decline in the proportion of deputy ministers that have five or more years experience as deputy ministers. The decline started in the early 1960s. It appeared to be reversing towards the end of the 1970s, but began another plunge in 1980 that by 1987 had left only a few deputy ministers with broad experience.

Average figures for "total experience as a deputy minister" tell a similar story. In 1966 the average was 5.3 years. In 1976 it was 4.0 years. In 1987 it was 3.4 years.

How long do ministers remain with departments?   With rare exceptions, ministers have seldom stayed for long periods in departments. Our survey did not reveal any pattern or trend in ministerial movements over the past three decades. In the 1960s, the average

---

FIGURE 6-3

DEPUTY MINISTERS
More than 5 years as a DM

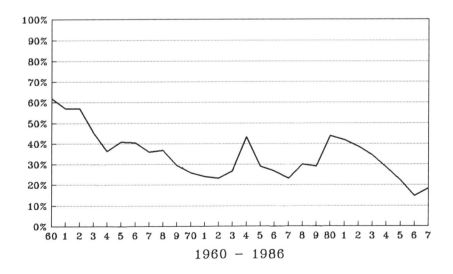

1960 − 1986

appointment of a minister lasted 1.8 years. In the 1970s, it rose to 2.2 years. In the 1980s it has fallen to 1.5 years.

How long do minister-deputy minister teams stay together?   In previous chapters we have emphasized the importance of the minister-deputy minister team. Despite this importance, the statistics show that with a few exceptions, the life of these teams has always been relatively brief. As illustrated by Figure 6-4, since 1960 the average team life has never risen above two years. For the four-year period 1984-1987, it averaged less than one year.

WHY HAS THE DURATION OF DEPUTY MINISTER APPOINTMENTS DECLINED ?

It is not within the scope of this study to examine all the political, personal, practical and sociological factors that gave rise to these statistics. Some explanation of the general forces that led to the

FIGURE 6-4

MINISTER / DEPUTY MINISTER
Team Tenure

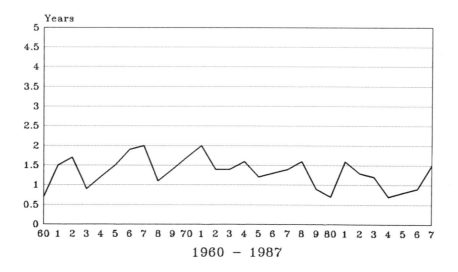

1960 — 1987

current situation is required, however, as a context for understanding the difficulty of making improvements.

A number of forces converged in the late 1960s to bring about a change in the value attached to functional knowledge of a department as opposed to knowledge of the government as a whole. The Royal Commission on Government Organization (1963), commonly referred to as the Glassco Commision, urged that more importance be attached to professional management and less to departmental expertise and policy development. At the same time, more importance was being placed on achieving overall coherence in the Government's program and on ensuring political control of the public service. Accordingly, emphasis was placed on appointing deputy ministers who were professional managers and knowledgeable about the work of government as a whole.

To some extent, this change was necessary. It helped governments achieve their priorities by raising the level of management expertise. An inevitable consequence, however, was a gradual swing towards appointment of deputy ministers who had extensive central agency experience. This swing was reinforced by the preoccupation of government with corporate planning processes during the 1970s.

Politics also underlies the tenure question. New governments change deputy ministers for a variety of reasons. Change may be an alternative to firing a deputy minister perceived to be too closely associated with a prior government's policy position. Removing an entrenched deputy minister may be a way to strengthen political control of a department. It may be used to inject new direction into a moribund department or to clean up a policy or administrative mess left over from a previous administration.

Governments may make changes to advance desirable management objectives, such as fairer representation of women or francophones at the deputy minister level. In 1976, 23 per cent of deputy ministers were francophones and 3 per cent were women. By 1987, considerable progress had occurred in this area: 33 per cent were francophones and 15 per cent were women.

Changes may be made for personal reasons. Ministers and deputy ministers may not get along. Deputy ministers may burn out from the stress of the job. Retirement is another factor. As a result of changes in the retirement provisions of the Public Service Superannuation Act in 1971, many deputy ministers choose to leave when they reach 55 years of age. Finally, deputy ministers are not all equally competent. Some have been removed for failing to carry out their duties adequately.

These are good reasons to change deputy ministers, and many of them are beyond the control of a government. Further, it is not always one single reason that causes a move. The research indicates that a combination of factors usually creates the need to move one or more deputy ministers.

It is likely that there will always be good reasons for moving deputy ministers. What ministers and deputy ministers have told us, however, is that there are also compelling reasons for letting deputy ministers (and ministers) stay longer in their departments.

IMPLICATIONS OF SHORT TENURE

Concerns about the short tenure of deputy ministers focused on three areas: the high risk of running a complex department with inadequate knowledge; the waste associated with breaking up an effective minister-deputy minister team; and the perceived loss of accountability caused by frequent rotation of deputy ministers.

The High Risk of Managing with Incomplete Information   As we discussed in Chapter 5, deputy ministers attach great importance to having detailed knowledge about their departments. If such knowledge is not gained through previous work in the department, deputy ministers must try to aquire it while carrying out their primary responsibilities.

Once deputy ministers are appointed, the time available for learning about the department (as opposed to the amount of time required to manage a pressing agenda) is limited. The result is that deputy ministers feel uncomfortable with their role as co-ordinator of the department's diverse areas of activity. As the senior executive, their role is to take an enormous quantity of fragmented information produced by the department, put it into the context of political and external factors, and draw broad conclusions about potential risks and opportunities. This task cannot be carried out successfully if the deputy minister does not have a good knowledge of the department. The requirement to address issues in a very short time frame means that deputy ministers often rely extensively on individual functional groups for the management of issues. Over time, this can lead to dissolution of links among the various groups and to the balkanization effect mentioned in Chapter 5.

Short tenure means that deputy ministers may learn about the current high-profile areas but may be unable to learn enough about the department in a broad sense to detect potential problems with the department's continuing operations and responsibilities. Consequently they are less able to protect a minister from errors or enable a minister to take advantage of opportunities. For many deputy ministers, a tenure of less than two or three years in a department where they have had no previous experience means that they will not have a chance to become fully effective before they leave their post.

Breaking Up the Team   Ministers and chief political aides are concerned about the tenure of deputy ministers. A significant amount of effort is expended by the minister, the minister's staff and the deputy minister in making the interpersonal and administrative arrangements necessary to work as a team.

Some ministers may never trust public servants as a group, but the evidence indicates that experienced ministers tend to trust at least their own deputy minister, even if they don't trust any of the others. This selective bonding may be a function of human nature, but given the critical importance of the minister-deputy minister relationship, it should be used to advantage.

The Moving Target   Our interviews with parliamentarians and our review of parliamentary committee proceedings revealed a persistent concern about the tenure of senior officials in general and deputy ministers in particular. Committee members express frustration when the official who was in place at the time an incident occurred has been moved and replaced by another by the time the committee investigates the incident. The problem arises because committees normally consider audits or reports dealing with circumstances that are at least a few months old. Officials may leave before they have to answer for their actions. The following excerpt from a committee's proceedings is typical of the view of many committee members. The comments are directed at a newly appointed deputy minister of the Department of Regional Industrial Expansion. This department had three deputy ministers in the previous three years:

"When your desk seems to be rotating quite frequently, how do we hold anyone accountable? Have you any suggestions, because this is a matter of frustration, I think, for this committee and for a lot of other people as to how in heaven's name do we actually say, `the buck stops here', when the person who was sitting in that seat has been gone for a few months, or a year, or whatever it is." [2]

IMPLICATIONS OF LONG TENURE

The two most common concerns expressed about overly long tenure for deputy ministers were burnout, caused by the high-stress nature of the job, and the potential loss of objectivity resulting from excessive identification with the department.

Burnout   The job of deputy minister is extremely demanding, both physically and mentally. It requires energy, enthusiasm, toughness, resilience, and imagination at levels that cannot be sustained indefinitely. One ex-deputy minister expressed what we found to be a common feeling:

"During my entire time as deputy minister I did not feel that I was able to leave Ottawa, because the Minister might call and I would let him down if I wasn't there. After a few years, I couldn't take it anymore. I had to give up my post as deputy minister."

Loss of Objectivity   While most ministers were generally confident that their deputy ministers would do their best to serve every minister with the expected degree of objectivity, some expressed concerns about deputies that remained with a particular department too long, and were therefore too committed to existing policies.

IMPLICATIONS OF THE LOSS OF SENIOR DEPUTY MINISTERS

Figure 6-3 shows that the number of experienced deputy ministers has gradually diminished over the past three decades. Deputy ministers fear that as such individuals leave, several significant things are lost that would otherwise have contributed to the quality of advice provided to ministers and to the management capability of the public service.

The public service loses role models. Many deputy ministers said that they learned how to be deputy ministers by observing the experienced deputy ministers of the 1960s and early 1970s:

"I am really part of the `learn by watching' school of deputy minister development. Deputy ministers develop from assistant deputy ministers watching good deputy ministers work. I have two deputy minister role models. In many situations I ask myself what these two people would do with this type of problem. It helps me a lot and keeps me focused on the fundamentals. Some aspects of the job just cannot be written down. I don't know how people can operate as deputy ministers without the benefit of these types of role models."

The second is the loss of informal advisers. Many deputy ministers said that they place great value on the presence of senior deputy ministers whom they could call for advice on tough decisions.

The third is the loss of knowledge. At this time, there are very few senior public servants who have any historical perspective on issues. One senior deputy minister told of a recent, frustrating encounter with this problem:

"I was chairing a meeting of deputy ministers on a current issue that was similar to an issue that a previous government had dealt with. There was no one at the table who could help ministers to learn from the previous experience. Yet, the Government could have benefited significantly from such expertise."

6.2   DEVELOPMENT AND TENURE OF CHIEF EXECUTIVE OFFICERS

In Chapter 5, the observation was made that differences in the accountability systems of deputy ministers and CEOs may preclude a direct transfer of management techniques between the private and public sectors. One area where I believe that a beneficial transfer to the public sector may be made is human resource management.

Deputy ministers and chief executive officers (CEOs) are both highly valuable organizational resources, but there is a stark contrast between how the private and public sectors manage questions of tenure and career management for senior executives. Current literature suggests that a great deal of effort is expended on development, selection and retention of CEOs.[3] We pursued this theme in our 21 interviews with Canadian CEOs. We asked CEOs what steps they or their board took to select the next CEO. Were CEOs from inside the company preferred? How were they identified? How were they developed? If the new CEO came from outside the company, what steps were taken to ensure continuity with the previous CEO?

IDENTIFICATION AND DEVELOPMENT OF POTENTIAL CEOs

Observers of the CEO succession process state that although the number of CEOs appointed from outside has increased in recent years, the majority of companies still prefer to appoint from within the organization. This observation was borne out in our interviews. Early identification of people with high potential was seen by CEOs as a vital task for the organization:

"We spend a great deal of time bringing up our promising managers. We have an annual manpower planning process that involves assessments by supervisors and personal counselling during an interview. A form is completed that includes developmental recommendations. From these forms are made the training and movement plans for the next year. This is not considered to be an administrative task; it is part of development of the business. The process is almost entirely driven and implemented by the management team."

Most companies had a formal process similar to this one. One CEO told us of a major corporation in the United States that uses the concept of "corporate resource". Once an individual is identified as having high potential, that individual is formally classified as a corporate resource. Corporate resource individuals cannot be moved within the company without the approval of the chairman of the board.

CEOs spend a significant amount of time identifying and developing these people. One CEO of a company with about 4,000 employees described his involvement in the the process:

> *"To make sure the system is working, I meet with each of the people reporting to me and their team of managers to go over the results of the assessment process. During the December through February time period, fully 25 per cent of my time is spent on this activity. All of this comes together in a 30-minute presentation each year to the Board of Directors. I go through a review of each of the people working for me and I review the high potential ones lower in the company. This is a modified version of the system used in the parent company. The CEO of that company personally reviews the assessments of all persons above a certain level. That's about 400 people. If you don't have a strong team of people you're not on first base."*

Many of the CEOs we spoke with were aware that they had been identified early in their careers as a potential senior executive. One had been notified by senior management that he was "being watched" nearly 20 years before his appointment as CEO.

Once companies have identified their high flyers, they take positive steps to ensure that these employees get the development and exposure they need to advance to senior positions. CEOs mentioned two principal methods of achieving this goal. The first, and most formal, was moving people around and sending them on training courses:

> *"I have a couple of people right now who might be CEO in few years. You have to move them around to see if they can be successful in a different role than they were in. It also broadens their experience. We now have our finance director as manager of engineering. Regarding training, I've already had 30 people on the American Management Course, and we send people to Stanford. We also have someone going full time, on salary, to get an MBA."*

The second method is less formal. One CEO described it this way:

> *"You can always tell who are the high flyers in the company, because they keep turning up in meetings where they have no real function except to listen. I try to bring the up and comers to meetings, even if they don't really belong. It gives them exposure. One of my bosses used to do the same thing with me. He would call me into his office and then he would proceed to carry on with business as if I wasn't there. I sure learned a lot about his job that way."*

BACKGROUND OF CEOs: THE VALUE OF KNOWING THE BUSINESS

According to the CEOs we talked to, the reason boards of directors normally prefer to select CEOs from within the company is simple; they want a CEO that knows the business. Most CEOs agreed that the notion of a "professional manager", that is, a manager who can manage anything, is not valid.

> *"Nothing beats knowledge of the business. Anyone who thinks they can come from a soap company and run a seafood products company may have a big ego, but doesn't have much brains."*

> *"I've been reading that deputy ministers are changing jobs a lot in recent years. You can't do a job in conditions like that. I'm not a believer that you can manage anything. I can function in this environment, but I'm not sure I could go out and run Ford."*

Most of the CEOs we interviewed had a solid background in the company or at least in the business. This is consistent with the findings of a recent *Financial Post* survey.[4] The following quotations illustrate typical career patterns:

> *"I have been in this field since university and I have been in this company most of my career. My successor is relatively young in this field. He has been in the company for 16 years. In that time he has been in most of the major posts in the company."*

> *"My entire background is in this industry. That's 25 years. I started with our parent company as a plant design engineer. I then proceeded into the quality control side, and then into service. I was then moved into a strategic planning job, where among other things I was responsible for formation of this company."*

Sometimes a board must compromise on the requirement for knowledge of the business. Not all CEOs are appointed from within the company. A common reason for bringing in a CEO from outside is that the board wishes to change the direction of the company. Observers attribute the recent increase in the number of CEOs appointed from outside to the entry of companies into international markets. Boards need CEOs with a broader perspective than can be obtained within their company. This tendency to choose an outside CEO at a transition point in the company's life was illustrated in our interviews. Three of the companies that chose outside CEOs were diversifying into a new line of business or were taking the existing business into the international market. One CEO explained the circumstances for going outside for a new CEO:

> *"For several years we were a very static company with little growth. Until we started to acquire our competitors, we had little need for bringing people up. We are now in the process of training our people and identifying those that have high potential. We prefer to take people from inside, but because we were static for so long, we have too many hands-on people who do not have the skills to manage the new environment."*

Even when they hire from outside, boards remain concerned about retention, at a senior level, of knowledge of the business. All three companies took steps to retain the knowledge and experience of the outgoing CEO, usually by appointing him chairman of the board. Boards could also rely on their experience with the business to provide guidance to a new CEO.

CEO TENURE

CEOs were adamant that, once appointed, it was absolutely essential to remain in place long enough to become effective. Then they had to be permitted to function at that effective level for a number of years.

> *"You can't become effective overnight. In my view it takes two years to install a system of management and to get it running the way you want it."*

> *"I want people to know me, because when they know me they can understand my goals a lot better. It takes at least two years to get your goals across. It is also important that your customers and suppliers know you. The minimum time someone should be in this CEO job is five years."*

The average CEO tenure in the companies we surveyed was about nine years. CEOs were generally astonished at the turnover rate among deputy ministers and could not understand how government could operate under such conditions.

In summary, the practices of the private sector in the development, selection and retention of top executives hold valuable lessons for the public sector. Chapter 7 contains some specific recommendations aimed at improving the performance of the public sector in these areas.

6.3 ASSESSMENT OF DEPUTY MINISTER PERFORMANCE

The assessment process for deputy ministers is the formal method of evaluating the level at which deputy ministers are performing their roles. The variety of duties that deputy ministers may perform has been illustrated throughout this report. The difficulty of designing an assessment process that will accurately measure performance of these duties is formidable. It is well illustrated by the fact that the most common answer to the question, "What makes a successful deputy minister?" was "It all depends". The variation among ministers, deputies, departments, political climates and other factors produces a unique situation every time. The definition of success may change, depending on the perspective of the evaluator. Nonetheless, once a year the degree of success achieved by each deputy minister must be evaluated.

The nucleus of the deputy minister assessment process is the Committee of Senior Officials on Executive Personnel in the Public Service (COSO). COSO is an advisory body to the Secretary to the Cabinet. It deals with senior personnel management and related issues. The membership of COSO varies, but it is chaired by the Secretary to the Cabinet and includes the Secretary of the Treasury Board, the Comptroller General, the Chairman of the Public Service Commission and one or two other deputy ministers. Once a year, COSO reviews the performance of all deputy ministers. This review, together with the minister's evaluation of the deputy minister, constitutes the basis on which the Secretary to the Cabinet advises the Prime Minister as to the performance of a deputy minister. On the basis of this information, the Prime Minister decides on the performance rating of the deputy minister.

We asked deputy ministers how they felt about the formal assessment process. Is it fair? Could it be improved?

DEPUTY MINISTERS' VIEWS ON THE ASSESSMENT PROCESS

Deputy ministers expressed a wide range of opinions about the current assessment process. Most were satisfied that it was fair, but many felt that it measured the wrong factors, or at least not enough of the right factors.

The most common observation by deputy ministers was that it is extremely difficult to measure deputy minister performance. Traditional methods, involving assessment by the official's immediate superior, are simply not practical. The minister cannot fully evaluate the deputy minister's performance because he sees only a small part of what the deputy is doing. Nor is the Clerk of the Privy Council in a position to arrive at a detailed assessment of every deputy minister's performance. The Clerk has nearly 30 deputy ministers to assess in addition to officials in the Privy Council Office. It would not be unusual for the Clerk to spend an entire year without once focusing on the work of a given deputy minister, especially if the deputy minister's department is out of the mainstream of the current government agenda. In many cases, no one but the deputy minister can be fully aware of how he has carried out his responsibilities.

Many deputy ministers believe that because of this difficulty, any assessment system for deputy ministers can never be completely accurate. They feel, however, that the current system is for the most part a fair one, and that it produces a reasonable approximation of reality.

"The system is crude, rough and ready, and yet oddly enough, you can add refinements ad nauseum and you hardly ever change the results. In several years

as a deputy minister, I've never had a wildly inaccurate or ill-informed appraisal. The system of peer review is basically as good a way of appraising deputy ministers as you will find."

AREAS FOR IMPROVEMENT

Most deputy ministers support the COSO system but believe that some improvements could be made. One common observation relates to the lack of guidance upon taking charge of a department. Many deputy ministers felt that without an initial statement of expectations, any subsequent assessment could be off the mark:

"When you arrive as a deputy minister, it would be good to be told what the general expectations of your role are with respect to the management side of the organization. These would be good benchmarks for performance. If we believe in the value of our senior managers, we should have clearer expectations established by the centre and better feedback."

Deputy ministers who made this suggestion felt that the process of defining expectations should be co-ordinated, if not implemented, by the Associate Secretary to the Cabinet for Senior Appointments, an official in the Privy Council Office. Some deputy ministers felt that expectations and evaluation criteria should be tailored to each department and should be discussed and agreed upon between COSO and individual deputy ministers.

Many deputy ministers were concerned that assessments of their performance were too vulnerable to the 'random event'. They felt that because COSO has so little information on what they are doing, any assessment could easily be biased by negative media coverage of what may have been an isolated event. One deputy minister expressed it this way:

"I think that there are so many busy people doing so many things that when it comes down to judging people it becomes quite superficial. You can be on the upslope or the downslope too quickly because of hasty judgements. People have been badly hurt by this process."

Deputy ministers also expressed frustration about the lack of feedback on the results of their assessment, especially about where they could improve their performance.

JUDGEMENT: THE KEY FACTOR

Nearly all deputy ministers agreed that because of the complexity and ambiguity of their environment, the best performance indicator for virtually all their actions was the quality of their judgement.[5] As one deputy minister said:

"A deputy minister has to make decisions based on a blend of what was there before, the status quo, common sense, good judgement, departmental interests, the best interest of the minister, and the political needs of the moment. All of these go into making the decisions as opposed to saying `subsection 2, paragraph 9'."

As illustrated in Chapter 4, deputy ministers feel that they manage by radar. They must be able to live comfortably with a high degree of uncertainty and change. The success of the deputy minister depends heavily on a capacity to take signals from the environment, analyse them, make a judgement and take action. On many matters there is literally no one to whom the deputy minister can turn for a high-quality second opinion. Many vital decisions are unique — the situation has never arisen before and there are few, if any, points of reference for direction. Only the deputy mininster is privy to the full (albeit fragmented) range of information that must be considered, and decisions must often be made on very short notice.

In the presence of such a high degree of ambiguity, there is no substitute for quality of judgement. One deputy minister captured the qualitative nature of accountability for decision making in such an environment:

"Accountability for me is an art form. I have to balance the interests of the department's clients, advisory committees, the minister and the Government with my professional responsibilities to carry out the functions of the department under our act and the budgetary, organizational and other constraints that we must deal with. I have to use my knowledge and judgement to set priorities and directions for the organization."

Several deputy ministers felt that performance rating was based on a fragmented assessment of the department's performance on collective management demands, such as affirmative action, bilingualism, person year usage, etc. They felt that no one was rating them on the less tangible items. Deputy ministers were concerned that their performance on items often directly related to the quality of their judgement, such as service to the minister, progress on the mandate, and lack of public controversy, was being given short shrift.

The interviews with those familiar with the workings of the evaluation process, indicated that the assessors do try to take these factors into consideration. One senior deputy minister related an incident from a meeting where the performance of the deputy minister of a high-profile policy department was being assessed. A central agency review had indicated that the state of administration in the deputy minister's department was not healthy. The consensus of deputy ministers present, however, was that the deputy minister had been hired to move policy issues and was indisputably doing an excellent job. If administration was poor, get the deputy minister a good administrator to handle that side of the department — don't force her to spend more time on administration when the minister needs policy management.

The difficulty of assessing the less quantifiable dimensions of deputy minister performance is that it requires acceptance of a much broader concept of performance than is normally applied in formal evaluation systems. This concept takes into account the environment in which decisions are made, the personalities that the deputy minister must deal with, and current economic, political and administrative factors that affect the department. The only practical proxy for assessing this dimension of performance is the total package of results that have arisen as a consequence of the deputy minister's judgement.

6.4   PERSONAL VALUES: THE PUBLIC SERVICE ETHIC

The formal assessment process can provide ministers with some assurance that their deputy ministers are performing well. In addition, ministers have access to the deputy minister's personal file, which would contain previous evaluations and other performance indicators. While ministers do sometimes make use of these formal assessments, most said that they expect loyalty and top-rate performance simply because that is what a deputy minister in the Canadian public service is traditionally expected to provide. Deputy ministers believe that this faith in the entrenched values of senior public servants is well justified.

The box on the following page provides a summary of the feelings expressed by deputy ministers on the subject of their values.[6] Most deputy ministers consider the public service ethic to be the foundation upon which their accountability to the Prime Minister, the minister, Treasury Board and the Public Service Commission is built. As one deputy minister said:

> "I think that I have been more accountable because of the values that are imbued in the public service than because of the formal accountability structure."

The ethic is a source of great pride to deputy ministers. It is the basis of an internal drive that compels deputy ministers to act in an accountable fashion even when there is little likelihood they will actually be called to account for their actions.

A DEPUTY MINISTER TALKS ABOUT ETHICS

"Each and every deputy head must have a profound sense of morality and a complete feeling of being responsible and accountable to one's self. At all times, the deputy must be prepared to (but never have to) render a public account for what has been done; being proud to state that, to the best of his ability, within the resources provided, the complexity of restraints applied, the vagaries, contradictions and absence of direction received, he has done his best to manage his department or agency and to carry out or do what he believes has been legitimately expected of him by government, his minister, and his peers. It is this ethic which to me changes a basically suitable senior official into one who is truly able and meritorious, and it is this ethic which is the foundation of a public service which would be noted for its integrity and professionalism.

The route of specific, mechanistic accountability of deputy heads is not the route to follow to achieve a productive, efficient, creative public service with integrity, whose leadership is held in respect by the public, the politicians, the public service and the public service leadership itself. The most important determinant of the quality of the public service is, has been, and will continue to be the ethic of the senior public servants.

If this ethic is weak, then no amount or combination of other qualities will substitute, nor will any type, sort or format of specific accountability replace that fundamental shortcoming. In fact, the absence of such an ethic in an otherwise professionally competent senior public servant is dangerous. Its absence or weakness in a general sense throughout the senior levels of the public service, particularly at the deputy head level, sets the stage for sloth, inefficiency and, in the extreme, a public service riddled by graft and corruption.

Providing a deputy head does have this required ethic, he need not be outstanding in any other basic personal qualities, although he must have a combination of quality and variety which will enable him to put together a complete management team. With that view or perspective of his own conduct, the combination of his qualities and those of his senior officials should create a team which will provide high quality management for the department or agency."

"If I didn't feel a professional obligation to do things well, I would spend far fewer hours at my job and I would do it less well. I do that for myself. I don't do it because I'm accountable."

Deputy ministers rely on the public service ethic to help them fill in the gaps in direction from ministers or central agencies:

"I have a responsibility or accountability for the long-term capability of the department as an institution with a particular mandate or role in the country. I have a responsibility to move ahead of the immediate issues and be ready for the emerging issues or problems which will result from changes such as demographic shifts. In this department, there are issues that are coming down the road, and politicians are just not interested in them at this time. I have a responsibility for getting the more creative thinkers in the organization working on these issues so that we can support future ministers and so that the department is able to respond to problems within its mandate. If you didn't have a critical mass of deputy ministers who thought like this, you would be in trouble. This ethic does, however, need corporate reinforcement to survive."

Recently, a committee of deputy ministers and other senior officials conducted research for the purpose of defining the governing values of the federal public service. The resulting discussion paper, "Governing Values", explores the roots of the public service ethic and encourages further discussion and debate about it at all levels of the public service.[7]

6.5   WHERE WILL THE NEXT GENERATION OF DEPUTY MINISTERS COME FROM?

The interviews revealed discontent among assistant deputy ministers and younger deputy ministers with the working conditions of deputy ministers. There is a feeling that the risks and uncertainties of the job are such that fewer will want to be deputy ministers in the future. It is becoming more difficult to persuade a 44-year-old deputy minister to work 16-hour days, submit silently to character assassination in parliamentary committees and take home half the pay of peers in the private sector. Among those still willing to take the job, there is confusion about the qualifications required for appointment.

VIEWS OF ASSISTANT DEPUTY MINISTERS AND RECENTLY APPOINTED DEPUTY MINISTERS

Assistant deputy ministers, and their equivalents in central agencies, are one level below deputy ministers. At a similar point in the private sector, such as vice-president, they would have a very good idea of what their chances were of advancing to CEO. They would also have at least a fair idea of the chances of their peers. In some companies the succession would even be virtually confirmed one or two years before the incumbent CEO left.

In contrast, most of the assistant deputy ministers we interviewed had no idea what their chances were of becoming a deputy minister. Nor did they have a firm idea of anyone else's chances or even of the qualifications needed to advance to the deputy minister level. This feeling prevails despite efforts by the Public Service Commission to provide better career management information to senior managers.

Moreover, not all assistant deputy ministers see the top levels of the public service as a desirable career target.

> "While I used to advise young people that a job in the public service would be re-warding and challenging, I've changed my view. This is no longer such a desirable place to work. At the top levels there is half the pay of a comparable private sector job, there is little or no feedback on your performance, poor job security, and when you are dumped, there is no one to complain to. The working conditions in the public service have deteriorated."

This may be an extreme view, but it is disturbing to the extent that it echoes sentiments expressed by some deputy ministers regarding their actual working conditions.

6.6   FINDINGS: MANAGING THE DEPUTY MINISTER GROUP

Ministers and deputy ministers believe that the ability of deputy ministers to carry out their duties may be seriously jeopardized by a lack of knowledge about their department. Despite this concern, most deputy ministers are appointed to departments in which they have no previous experience. There is little to be gained by holding deputy ministers accountable for programs and activities they do not fully understand. Certainly, if errors are made, the deputy minister can be reprimanded, or even fired, but the net result is that ministers are unable to implement their agendas, employees are demoralized, and the careers of otherwise excellent individuals are ruined.

This lack of knowledge about departments is compounded by the brief duration of deputy minister appointments. Most deputy ministers felt that they could have accomplished much more if they had been left in their departments longer. The interviews showed that they felt a minimum of three years was required in order to reach their full potential for effectiveness.

The number of experienced (i.e., more than five years as a deputy minister) deputy ministers in the public service has decreased to the point where it may affect the quality of some government decisions. For a variety of reasons, including job conditions and changing career expectations, deputy ministers are leaving the public service after only one or two deputy minister apppointments. This means that there are fewer experienced individuals that the government can call upon for advice on issues that require some historical perspective for full understanding.

Deputy ministers believe that the process for assessing their performance is a fair one, as long as it includes consideration of the intangible results of their work. Ministers can rely on a combination of this system and the deputy minister's past performance record to justify their trust in the deputy ministers's competence. They feel that the most reliable basis upon which ministers can base their trust of a deputy minister's loyalty is the public service ethic. They are certain that this ethic is strong and influential in the deputy minister group.

CHAPTER 7 CONCLUSIONS AND RECOMMENDATIONS

I believe strongly that departments must be under firm political control and direction to preserve democratic government. Deputy ministers must be responsive to the direction of ministers and manage departments effectively on their behalf.

The study shows that the best means to ensure that deputy ministers are kept accountable to ministers and the Government is to have a good working relationship between ministers and deputy ministers based on their respective political and management roles and responsibilities. This has always been difficult to achieve because of the difficulty of developing the trust that is the essential foundation of such a relationship. However, it is becoming even more difficult for ministers and deputy minister to work effectively together. This is the result of increasing complexity and confusion with respect to the role and accountability requirements of deputy ministers, rapid change in minister-deputy minister teams, and a decline in the amount of experience deputy ministers have in their departments.

If governments do not support and reinforce the working partnership between ministers and deputy ministers, there is a distinct possibility that the nucleus or core of the accountability system of deputy ministers will be gravely damaged. If this occurs ministers will have greater difficulty carrying out their essential functions and deputy ministers will have more difficulty responding to the direction of ministers. In addition, deputy ministers will face an increasing number of obstacles to ensuring that departments support ministers and the Government. Without strong minister-deputy minister teams, governments will find it increasingly difficult to govern effectively.

In the remainder of this chapter, I set out the three major conclusions of this study as well as several recommendations that I think are necessary for keeping deputy ministers accountable.

7.1 CONCLUSIONS

CONCLUSION 1:   The accountability system for deputy ministers is complex, but it is basically sound and workable.

The multiple accountability obligations and responsibilities of deputy ministers create a complex and sometimes difficult management environment. However, among the more than 150 minister-deputy minister teams that our interviewees had worked in, there was not one serious suggestion that a minister could not hold a deputy minister accountable or that a deputy minister did not feel accountable to a minister. Similarly, Treasury Board and Public Service Commission officials were generally satisfied that deputy ministers could be held accountable for the responsibilities that these two bodies had conferred on them. There was also no doubt in anyone's mind that the Prime Minister could hold deputy ministers to account.

Deputy ministers are able to manage effectively within this environment as long as there is a good minister-deputy minister working relationship based on trust, a clear agenda, a good understanding of their respective roles, open communication and complementary skills.

THE COMPLEX WORKING ENVIRONMENT OF DEPUTY MINISTERS

The complexity, ambiguity and uncertainty of the deputy minister's working environment is inevitable in modern government. I believe that there is little likelihood that this working environment can be simplified through institutional changes. The challenge that deputy ministers face is how to work effectively in an environment where they have multiple accountability relationships and are dependent on so many groups for support, approval, or access to the decision-making process.

To support the minister effectively within this complex management environment, deputy ministers have to be able to balance their accountability to the minister:

——   with their accountability obligations to the Prime Minister, the Treasury Board, and the Public Service Commission for collective management;

——   with the sense of responsibility they feel to other groups such as clients and their answerability requirements to parliamentary committees; and

―――   with their responsibility to provide leadership and management direction to the department.

To do this, they have to manage the interface between the minister, the department, and the external environment. This type of management requires a considerable range of abilities and a strong public service ethic, as well as a good knowledge of government and the policies, programs and operations of the department.

Having said that the accountability system is sound and workable, I will go on to point out that there are some conditions under which it works best. The most important of these conditions is the subject of my second conclusion.

CONCLUSION 2: The accountability system for deputy ministers works best when ministers and deputy ministers understand their respective roles and can form an effective relationship that is based on trust.

In Chapter 4, I suggested that ministers and deputy ministers share the narrow neck of an hourglass, where they are subject to constant pressures, demands and constraints. The minister-deputy minister team must work within the context of overall government priorities and directions as well as central management and decision-making processes. They have to deal with the demands of clients, parliamentarians, and agencies and cope with changes in policies, priorities and management practices. Finally, they have to manage and direct large multi-program departments and respond to the requirements of staff for direction and leadership.

When the political environment of a department is uncertain and/or the department is very complex, it is even more important that ministers and deputy ministers work effectively as a team. With a good working relationship and the necessary skills, an effective minister-deputy minister team can review and respond to problems, adapt to the changing political milieu, and at the same time provide sufficient direction to the department to ensure that its day-to-day work is carried out.

Deputy ministers can carry out their major functions within the complex institutional framework of the federal government as long as ministers, the Prime Minister, central agencies, parliamentarians and other groups understand the basic reporting relationships and responsibilities that make up the system. Multiple accountabilities and diverse responsibilities become a problem when a deputy minister cannot develop a mutual understanding with a minister about their role and accountability requirements.

In the past fifteen years or more the views of ministers and deputy ministers about the importance of the partnership between ministers and deputy minister have not changed. The overwhelming conclusion of my study of more than 150 minister-deputy minister teams is that this working relationship is the most critical factor in determining whether ministers and deputy ministers carry out their functions effectively.

THE MINISTER-DEPUTY MINISTER WORKING RELATIONSHIP: KEY TO DEPUTY MINISTER ACCOUNTABILITY

When the minister-deputy minister working relationship is strong, deputy ministers can support the minister and the Government to establish and implement their agendas. They can contribute to effective departmental and collective management, balance their various accountability obligations, and meet their obligation to Parliament. In Chapters 2 and 4 we showed how experienced ministers, complemented by deputy ministers with a strong knowledge of the department and government, can formulate a clear agenda and implement it despite the considerable complexity and uncertainty of the political and management environment.[1]

Without a healthy working relationship with a deputy minister, ministers tend to ignore or mistrust the department. They do not tap the skills or advice available. They may use their chief political aide to run the department. This inevitably results in a poorly informed minister or a minister who is unable to carry out his or her political responsibilities effectively. A poor working relationship with the deputy minister and the department is at the root of many a minister's career disaster. If a deputy minister cannot communicate with the minister, or the minister fails to establish an agenda, the deputy minister faces major problems trying to support the minister, provide direction to the department, or respond to central agency direction.

Seventy per cent of ministers and deputy ministers in the teams we studied were able to establish good working relationships. Ministers had no difficulties holding their deputy ministers accountable to them and achieving the required support of the department. Deputy ministers were able to work well with their ministers and to reconcile their multiple accountability requirements. In such instances, we found that the deputy minister was able to work much more effectively with directors general and assistant deputy ministers because there was a common understanding of the minister's priorities and how the minister should be supported.

In the remaining 30 per cent of the cases, problems led on occasion to the removal of the deputy minister, the minister or both. In many cases these poor working relationships resulted in poor decisions or mistakes that embarrassed a Government.

The best way of ensuring that deputy ministers are accountable to ministers and the Government is to encourage and foster an effective working relationship between ministers and deputy ministers. However, there are many forces at work that can prevent this from happening. This brings me to my third conclusion.

CONCLUSION 3: The accountability system for deputy ministers has been made increasingly complex over the past two decades. As a result, effective working relationships between ministers and deputy ministers have become more difficult to establish and maintain.

Despite the enormous importance attached to ministerial responsibility and the accountability of deputy ministers to ministers in the parliamentary system, many of the institutional changes that have taken place in the past 20 years have made it more difficult for ministers and deputy ministers to work together effectively.

The most vulnerable part of the current accountability system for deputy ministers is the accountability of deputy ministers to ministers. By comparison, the accountability of deputy ministers to the Prime Minister, to the Public Service Commission and to Treasury Board is functioning well.

Three factors have made it more difficult for ministers and deputy ministers to establish an effective working relationship: confusion about the respective roles of ministers and deputy ministers; the short length of time ministers and deputy ministers work together; and a steady reduction in the level of departmental knowledge and experience among deputy ministers.

Confusion of Roles Most of the institutional changes that have occurred in the past 15 years have led to increasing confusion about the roles of ministers and deputy ministers. Governments have responded to priorities such as improving collective management by developing central policy and management processes; providing a greater role for backbenchers in Parliament through parliamentary reform; and ensuring increased representation of regions or groups in Cabinet through ministers of state. However, the pursuit of these priorities has added to the complexity of the accountability system and weakened the critical relationship between ministers and deputy ministers.

At this point in the evolution of the federal accountability system it is important to clarify the roles and accountability obligations of deputy ministers. If the principles of our parliamentary form of government are to be maintained, care must be taken to ensure that fundamental concepts of ministerial responsibility and the accountability of deputy ministers to ministers are well understood and safeguarded.

Short Tenure of Minister-Deputy Minister Teams   It takes time to establish an effective working relationship. Yet, it is not unusual for the minister of a department to change every year to eighteen months, and in the last couple of years deputy ministers averaged only about 2 years in a department. During the mid-1980s, minister-deputy minister teams were remaining in place for an average of less than a year.

Most ministers and deputy ministers said that it took at least three months to establish an effective working relationship and a minimum of six months to feel comfortable with the policies and programs of a new department. There is no doubt that ministers and deputy ministers get used to working with each other and become much stronger teams after their first year together. Few minister-deputy minister teams have this opportunity. In this state of constant change, deputy ministers have to spend most of their time learning about the department, developing a working relationship with the minister, or acting as a broker between the minister, the minister of state and the chief of staff.

Decrease in the Experience of Deputy Ministers in Their Departments   To a large extent, the integrity of the accountability system depends on deputy ministers with:

—— the wisdom to know when to advise the minister;

—— the insight to determine how best to assist the minister to implement his or her agenda;

—— the ability to assess the management, administrative and political implications of various proposals;

—— the sense to consult, co-ordinate and co-operate with the relevant actors;

—— the experience to know when central agency directions or demands from other groups take precedence over departmental management requirements and when they do not; and

—— the knowledge to guide large, multi-program departments with various competing objectives.

The research results indicate that deputy ministers have extensive policy skills and are familiar with the collective management requirements of the government. They can thus meet most of the foregoing list of requirements. However, the research also indicates that the federal government is losing the benefits of a productive division of labour between ministers who provide political direction and deputy ministers who are knowledgeable about departments, because deputy ministers often do not know their departments as well as they should.[2]

Deputy ministers require general policy and management skills as well as the specific skills to manage their departments. A deputy minister who is successful in one department will not necessarily be successful in another. Chapters 5 and 6 show that deputy ministers seldom have in-depth knowledge of a department when they are appointed, and they do not stay much longer than ministers. Thus, it is more and more difficult for them to provide the necessary leadership and direction to departments.

7.2   RECOMMENDATIONS

Unlike other reports on accountability, this one does not recommend a new management system or accountability process. I am not promoting institutional change, new central agencies or watchdog organizations. I do not recommend transplanting concepts such as the British accounting officer from other countries or imitating the private sector by establishing a bottom-line approach to measuring performance. Finally, I have not succumbed to the temptation to build on proposals by others to politicize the public service or increase the accountability of deputy ministers to Parliament. What the research has done is to reaffirm the importance of the conventions of our parliamentary system and to reaffirm the conditions necessary for accountable and responsible government.

I have rejected three specific proposals made over the past decade to change the accountability system of deputy ministers. First is the proposal to politicize the appointment of deputy ministers, or even worse, appointments to other levels of the public service.[3] Politicization would lead to a fundamental and probably irreversible change in the accountability of deputy ministers. The partisan appointment of deputy ministers would ultimately deprive ministers and the Government of deputy ministers with the necessary abilities, skills, judgement and ethics to do their jobs. As recent studies in the United States have indicated, politicization would lead inevitably to a substantial deterioration in the knowledge of senior executives about government generally and about individual departments. Such politicization would lead to patronage appointments; patronage systems are not designed to search out the best and the brightest.[4]

The second proposal I have rejected is what I call the parallel accountability of deputy ministers to parliamentary committees. This proposal has the potential to reduce the degree of control ministers exercise over their departments.[5] Although I believe strongly that deputy ministers should be answerable to Parliament on behalf of ministers, they cannot be accountable to both parliamentary committees and ministers.[6] Unless deputy ministers are clearly accountable to ministers for all matters, it will be very difficult for ministers to hold deputy ministers and departments accountable to them. And it will be increasingly difficult for Parliament to hold ministers responsible for their departments.[7] Ministers should always retain the right to instruct deputy ministers and public officials on how to represent them before Parliament and should be prepared to intervene when necessary with parliamentary committees to explain their policy or management directions.

Another proposal put forward to improve the accountability system is to increase central agency controls and make deputy ministers more accountable for specific management systems and processes.[8] The fallacy of this approach is illustrated in Chapter 4. Detailed central controls result in fragmented accountability. They tend to create government by rules instead of performance and management by processes rather than results. Given the major differences in the management requirements of various departments, centrally pre-scribed management systems and processes can lead to less effective department management. Studies in the United Kingdom and the United States and recent reports by the Auditor General of Canada have illustrated that extensive central controls lead not only to reduced productivity but also to diffused accountability.[9]

The best means of achieving responsive and effective government is by having ministers provide the political direction to departments supported by capable deputy ministers. Elaborate central systems, parliamentary review mechanisms or watchdog agencies can lead to a weakening of the accountability system, and ultimately they cannot make up for a weak minister, an incompetent deputy minister, or a poor minister-deputy minister working relationship.

REQUIREMENTS FOR A HEALTHY ACCOUNTABILITY SYSTEM FOR DEPUTY MINISTERS

For deputy ministers to be accountable to ministers and to develop the kind of working relationships required for responsive and effective government, five components are essential:

1. The accountability of deputy ministers to ministers has to be clear and well understood by all the major players involved in the system.

2. Deputy ministers have to be able to establish a good working relationship with ministers based on a clear understanding of their respective roles and a shared agenda.

3. Deputy ministers have to have the authority and flexibility to manage the department to support the minister's agenda and priorities within the context of government-wide management and policy requirements.

4. Deputy ministers must have the knowledge, experience, and public service ethic to advise and support a minister and manage a department.

5. There has to be a realistic and credible performance assessment system and career development system for deputy ministers to ensure that ministers and the Government have deputy ministers with the capabilities needed for the job and perform their functions effectively.

The recommendations address these requirements for a workable accountability system for deputy ministers. In presenting these recommendations, I have tried to maintain the basic principles of our parliamentary system while adapting to the realities of modern government. I have tried to keep deputy ministers accountable to ministers and to the Government and ensure that deputy ministers are competent to carry out their jobs effectively.

The recommendations aim to strengthen the capacity of ministers to direct their departments and hold their deputy ministers accountable. They outline the conditions necessary for ministers and deputy ministers to develop strong working relationships. They are also intended to ensure that a cadre of qualified public servants is available to the Government for deputy minister appointments.

TEN AREAS OF RECOMMENDATIONS

1. The accountability system of deputy ministers

2. The requirements for a good minister-deputy minister working relationship

3. The role of ministers of state

4. The role of chief of staff

5. The Increased Ministerial Authority and Accountability (IMAA) initiative

6. The department knowledge and tenure of deputy ministers

7. The experience level of deputy ministers

8. Career and succession planning

9. The need for a national centre for executive development

10. The performance appraisal system for deputy ministers

RECOMMENDATIONS ON THE ACCOUNTABILITY SYSTEM OF DEPUTY MINISTERS

1. ACCOUNTABILITY SYSTEM: The federal government should reaffirm and reinforce the accountability of deputy ministers to ministers and in the future, changes by governments or Parliament should not be allowed to jeopardize this critical accountability relationship.

It is essential that parliamentarians, ministers, deputy ministers and other public servants clearly understand the accountability system. It is particularly important that ministers and deputy ministers understand their respective roles and relationships and the need to work together.

The Need for a Consolidated Description of the Accountability Requirements of Deputy Ministers

One way to clarify the overall accountability system is through a government-endorsed description of the role and accountability requirements of deputy ministers. Because of the institutional complexity of the federal government, the Privy Council Office should continually restate the major principles and relationships that make up the accountability system of deputy ministers. As a result of recent changes, including parliamentary reforms and the increased use of ministers of state, it is important that this be done now.

To address the same problem, the Secretary to the Cabinet in Britain recently issued two major statements intended to provide a "clear definitive statement of the duties and responsibilities of civil servants in their relationships with ministers, of their accountability to Ministers, and of the relationship between that and the responsibilities and accountability of ministers to Parliament."[10]

The Privy Council Office should update and consolidate its various statements on the role and accountability of deputy ministers in a comprehensive and readable document. The statement should be based on this report as well as several excellent reports produced by the Privy Council Office, such as "Responsibility in the Constitution" (1979),[11] "The Office of Deputy Minister"[12] and the guidelines explaining the responsibilities of deputy ministers testifying before parliamentary committees and the relationships among ministers, officials and parliamentarians.[13] Such a document should distinguish clearly between the accountability, answerability and management responsibility relationships of deputy ministers. It would provide an important source of direction to deputy ministers about their functions and responsibilities and familiarize ministers and parliamentarians with the role of deputy ministers.

This document, along with other key documents produced by the Privy Council Office concerning the roles and responsibilities of deputy ministers as well as documents providing general guidance to ministers, should be widely distributed to parliamentarians, the media, universities and the public. In addition, the Privy Council Office should play a more active role in publishing reports, documents and speeches that could contribute to a better appreciation of the issues surrounding the structure and functioning of the federal government.

Briefings and Orientation Programs

Documents are not enough. The Privy Council Office has been briefing new ministers for the past year based on some of the documents they have produced on the roles of ministers and deputy ministers. They have also provided written guidance to ministers on the nature of their responsibilities. These briefings help ministers understand their collective and individual responsibilities and the role of their deputy minister. PCO has been conducting similar briefings for deputy ministers. This mechanism is tailor-made for helping ministers and deputy ministers understand their roles and responsibilities.[14]

To give parliamentarians an opportunity to familiarize themselves with the roles of ministers, deputy ministers and parliamentary committees, it is suggested that Parliament include a major component on the accountability system in existing orientation programs for parliamentarians.

To assist other senior executives and public servants to understand the nature of the accountability system, a major component of its public service management courses should be devoted to explaining how the accountability system works.

Actions by the Prime Minister, Secretary to the Cabinet, Ministers and Deputy Ministers

One should never underestimate the importance of continually reinforcing the principles of the accountability system of deputy ministers through government actions or behaviour. A statement by the Prime Minister in Parliament or in Cabinet making it clear what he expects of deputy ministers is very important in reinforcing the basic principles of the accountability system. A minister who explains the role of the deputy minister to a parliamentary committee can help to clarify the accountability of deputy ministers. It is also important for the Secretary to the Cabinet and deputy ministers to remind public servants regularly of their responsibilities and how they should be carried out.

RECOMMENDATIONS CONCERNING THE MINISTER-DEPUTY MINISTER WORKING RELATIONSHIP

2. MINISTER-DEPUTY MINISTER WORKING RELATIONSHIP: The federal government must place a higher priority on the establishment of strong working relationships between ministers and deputy ministers and should establish an objective of two years as the minimum time that ministers and deputy ministers should work together.

There are four major ways to promote the minister-deputy minister working relationship: supporting ministers to carry out their responsibilities; increasing the length of time ministers and deputy ministers work together as a team; clarifying the role of deputy ministers with respect to ministers of state; and facilitating a professional working relationship between the minister, deputy minister and chief political aide.

To achieve greater continuity in minister-deputy minister teams, deputy ministers and ministers must be moved less frequently. It is very difficult to avoid frequent changes of ministers. Elections, the need to promote and move ministers, and the requirement to change ministers to carry out the Government's agenda means that it is unlikely that the average tenure of ministers will ever be more than two years. To increase the tenure of minister-deputy minister teams to two years, the most promising area for improvement is to increase the tenure of deputy ministers.

Given the enormous challenges that ministers face in assuming responsibility for a new portfolio, they should not be denied a deputy minister who is knowledgeable about the department and who has had sufficient experience in the department to provide professional advice and support with respect to the policies, programs and operations of the department as well as the needs and views of clients.

This change will be difficult to accomplish. Shifts between portfolios are used to solve problems but the cost is not immediately evident. However, if the federal government cannot create greater stability in the working partnership between ministers and deputy ministers, constant change will continue to exact high costs in terms of the performance of ministers and deputy ministers. To put it simply, a higher value must be placed on continuity relative to the value placed on achieving other objectives.

In addition to increasing the tenure of minister-deputy minister teams, the federal government should try to ensure that ministers and deputy ministers complement each other in terms of the management style, knowledge and skills required to direct a given department and achieve government priorities. However, there is no sense in maintaining a flawed relationship for the sake of continuity. Such problems should be attended to as quickly as possible. If the problem cannot be solved, the team should be split up.

3. MINISTERS OF STATE: The federal government should ensure that the responsibilities of ministers of state are clear and that their relationship to ministers and deputy ministers is understood.

When ministers of state are appointed, the Government should make it clear what role is expected of them and what authorities they have. This can be done in the mandate letter provided to the minister of the department by the Prime Minister. To ensure that ministers and ministers of state quickly determine their respective roles and responsibilities, it is suggested that within three months of their appointment, ministers forward to the Prime Minister a description of the roles, responsibilities and authorities that have been agreed to with the minister of state.

Since the minister and minister of state will need to work together, it is important that they be compatible. Thus, ministers should have an important role in determining whether they will have a minister or state and who it will be. It is also essential that ministers of state understand clearly their role with respect to the deputy minister of the department. This should be agreed upon between the minister and minister of state when discussing their respective responsibilities.

4. CHIEF POLITICAL AIDES: The Prime Minister's Office should establish a selection, training and development program to ensure the Government has well qualified chief political aides.

The concept of a chief political aide (i.e., chiefs of staff, executive assistants or senior policy advisers to ministers under various governments) does not pose basic problems for the accountability of deputy ministers to ministers. The main challenge is to ensure that competent chief political aides are appointed that can support ministers and the Government effectively and that they complement the minister-deputy minister team.

The Prime Minister's Office should develop an eligibility list of potential chief political aides who meet the following requirements:

—— personal compatibility and rapport with a minister and ability to assist a minister in developing and managing his or her agenda;

—— good political judgement and the talent to provide politically partisan advice and support to the minister and to assess the political implications of proposals brought forward by the minister or department;

—— capability to work within the political networks of the Government and the caucus and with the clientele of the department; and

—— ability to manage the minister's office and work co-operatively with the deputy minister and senior department officials.

In addition to these requirements, candidates who already have a good knowledge of government or a particular policy field are a distinct asset.

The federal government should also review the qualifications and skills required for chief political aides to ministers of major departments as compared to ministers of other departments and ministers of state. It should consider the need for a two or three-level classification system that recognizes the differences in these jobs, provides for some career advancement and enables political advisers to assume progressive levels of responsibility.

RECOMMENDATIONS ON THE AUTHORITY OF MINISTERS AND DEPUTY MINISTERS FOR MANAGING DEPARTMENTS

5. INCREASED MINISTERIAL AUTHORITY AND ACCOUNTABILITY (IMAA): The Government should ensure that the critical conditions required to implement IMAA are in place and should carry out its intention to shift the role of the Treasury

Board from detailed functional and financial control to the provision of overall management guidelines to departments and the review of their performance.

The proposals put forward by the Treasury Board to increase ministerial authority and accountability can help ministers and deputy ministers obtain the flexibility they need to manage and direct departments more effectively. This will enable deputy ministers to be more responsive to ministers in the management of departments.

IMAA aims to streamline central agency requirements and establish a clearer basis of authority for holding deputy ministers accountable for department management and the achievement of collective management priorities.

Through agreements between the Treasury Board and departments, IMAA provides an opportunity to clarify the collective management requirements that departments have to deal with and to link them specifically to department management requirements. By conducting annual and three-year reviews of the performance of departments under the IMAA agreements, a clearer accountability regime will be established between departments and Treasury Board.

Implementing Increased Ministerial Authority and Accountability

The full implementation of IMAA would be a major achievement, but it will not be easy. IMAA represents an important step forward in reconciling collective management requirements and department management requirements. Chapter 4 outlined the advantages of IMAA for improving the overall accountability of deputy ministers for department management and for avoiding some of the problems created by excessive central controls and fragmentation of accountability requirements.

The Treasury Board and Treasury Board Secretariat (TBS) recognize the challenges of implementing IMAA. Based on publications and statements by the President and Secretary of Treasury Board, as well as interviews with TBS executives, it is clear that there are at least five challenges to implementing IMAA successfully.

The Need for a Department Focus

To implement IMAA the Treasury Board must develop a department focus to complement its capacity in areas such as personnel, classification, and administrative policy. Without such a capability, TBS recognizes that it will have difficulties conducting reviews of department performance under IMAA agreements.

The challenge facing TBS in developing a department focus is considerable. It will have to develop a better understanding of the management requirements of individual departments and the ability to shape collective management requirements in light of department management challenges. This has not been done very well in the past. TBS is organized largely by functional groups such as personnel policy, administrative policy and official languages policy. Each group is mandated to focus on government-wide rather than departmental requirements. The principles of IMAA require a major shift in perspective and increased co-ordination of these groups with respect to the management of the IMAA agreements with each department.

The Responsibility of Ministers and Deputy Ministers for Department Management

The IMAA approach requires departments to accept increased responsibility for decision making without the comfort or irritant of Treasury Board approval. It requires deputy ministers to develop a more integrated approach to dealing with central agency requirements in their departments and to put management systems and practices in place to meet the requirements of the IMAA memorandum.

The Minister-Deputy Minister Working Relationship

The Treasury Board Secretariat recognizes that IMAA cannot work if ministers and deputy ministers do not agree on how to balance collective management requirements, ministerial priorities and department management requirements. As illustrated in Chapter 2, this will be difficult given rapid change in minister-deputy minister teams and the many factors that can disrupt their working relationship.

The Role of Treasury Board in IMAA

When the chips are down and claims are made that the contracting process is flawed or that new controls are required on travel expenditures or computers, the Treasury Board will have to resist the temptation to make yet another rule for all departments. The pressures on Treasury Board to continue to perform the kind of function it has carried out so well for many years will be considerable. Thus, it will take a lot of stamina and perseverance for the Treasury Board and its Secretariat to stay the course on IMAA.

The Accountability Sessions

IMAA implies a major change in the role of the Treasury Board with respect to departments. A key part of this change is the accountability sessions that are planned between the Treasury Board and the minister and deputy minister of a department. If the Treasury Board is not able to hold these accountability sessions there will be a tendency for Treasury Board to focus on specific problems and submissions as if the IMAA regime did not exist. If ministers and deputy ministers do not have an opportunity to explain their management approach to the Treasury Board, the Board will not be aware of the implications of various policies or controls on departments. Consequently, the political support for IMAA will be eroded.

RECOMMENDATIONS CONCERNING THE KNOWLEDGE AND SKILLS OF DEPUTY MINISTERS

6. DEPARTMENTAL KNOWLEDGE OF DEPUTY MINISTERS: The federal government should:

(a) place a higher priority on the appointment of deputy ministers who are knowledgeable about a department's policies, programs or field of activity and its management requirements; and

(b) establish a target of three years as the minimum tenure of a deputy minister in a department.

The emphasis placed on the minister-deputy minister working relationship is the most important aspect of this report. The evidence presented in this report illustrates that deputy ministers have to have special abilities to work with ministers and respond to their requirements. It also shows that the trends with respect to the tenure of deputy ministers have the potential to limit any possibility of developing the kind of partnership that is essential if ministers and deputy ministers are to work effectively together. Chapter 6 makes it clear that there are many reasons for the rapid rotation of deputy ministers. The conclusion that must be drawn, however, is that governments have gone too far in rotating deputy ministers and that they should place renewed emphasis on departmental expertise and knowledge in the selection and appointment of deputy ministers.

One of the assumptions that has shaped the policy of rotating deputy ministers is the notion that "a manager is a manager". This approach to management, which developed in the early 1970s, contended that management consisted of a body of general skills that a manager could apply to any organization. In the private sector this view has lost its lustre, but it still has some currency in government. Current practices in the private sector and the current management literature emphasize that there are significant differences between management jobs and that success requires a great deal of specific knowledge about particular organizations and how to manage them.[15] As a result of the view that deputy ministers are largely interchangeable, there has been little analysis of the requirements of managing in various kinds of departments. Such analysis would be useful in improving the selection of deputy ministers to head specific departments.

The adoption of this policy would have major implications for the development and appointment of deputy ministers. Under such a policy, every effort would be made to appoint qualified deputy ministers to a department where they had previous executive experience. As to appointments from outside the public service, the federal government would choose individuals already familiar with a department's programs and policies from a provincial or private sector perspective or who had knowledge of the department's professional field of expertise (law, taxation, health care).

7. EXPERIENCE OF DEPUTY MINISTERS: The Government should increase the overall level of experience of deputy ministers as deputy ministers to an average of four years (from its present level of about two years) and should make a special effort to retain several senior and successful deputy ministers who can provide continuity, expertise and advice to deputy ministers.

Chapter 6 showed that the overall level of experience of deputy ministers has declined rapidly in the past ten years. By the end of 1987, deputy ministers as a group had only 3.4 years average experience as deputy ministers.

The federal government has to manage its deputy minister group to ensure a proper balance between maintaining a constant supply of relatively young and capable deputy ministers from inside and outside the public service and fostering the development of a cadre of experienced deputy ministers who can assist and support less experienced deputy ministers to do their jobs effectively.

It is important to recognize the value of these senior deputy ministers to younger or future deputy ministers, to the promotion of a public service ethic, and as a source of advice for less experienced deputy ministers. It should be recognized that the value of these individuals is above and beyond their contribution to a given department.

Given the drastic decline in the overall experience base of the deputy minister community, the Government should make every effort to retain four or five of the most successful senior deputy ministers.

8. CAREER AND SUCCESSION PLANNING: The Government should develop a career planning and selection system for existing and prospective deputy ministers that trains them to assume responsibility for particular departments and central agency positions.

To achieve responsive and effective government, the federal government must ensure that it has a cadre of qualified deputy ministers who know their responsibilities, understand their accountability requirements and are capable of supporting ministers and the Government.

To develop and maintain deputy ministers of the requisite calibre the federal government must make a clear and sustained commitment to a professional public service and the requirement for capable non-partisan deputy ministers that can support ministers and the Government. This will require a better awareness of the complexities, difficulties, requirements and skills needed to be a good deputy minister and greater recognition of the value of deputy ministers to parliamentary government.

By comparison with the private sector, the federal government engages in little career or succession planning for deputy ministers. There are reasons for this; it is difficult to plan appointments where there are so many uncertainties about how deputy ministers will work with various ministers, and there are often constraints of time or availability when deputy ministers are being selected for particular departments. Notwithstanding these problems, it should be possible to improve succession planning in the federal public service and to use some of the techniques employed in the private sector for passing CEO responsibilities from one top executive to another.

In the private sector, top executives spend several years preparing for the job of CEO. The gradual handing over of responsibilities from one CEO to the next enables private companies to balance the need for change with the requirement to maintain continuity at the executive level.[16]

The career and succession planning system for deputy ministers should be managed by the Associate Secretary to the Cabinet on behalf of the Clerk of the Privy Council. I recognize that the selection of deputy ministers will be shaped by many factors, including the representation of various groups, personal suitability, availability, timing and interests. Regardless of the influence of these factors, the Government should make every effort to appoint the right person to the right position at the right time. If candidates and jobs are to be matched effectively, a career and succession planning system must be in place. The system should

—— Develop a profile for the specific policy and management skills required for each deputy minister position in the public service based on the experience of previous deputy ministers and an analysis of the nature of the department, its responsibilities, and its collective management requirements, as well as the specific requirements of ministers for support and advice in that particular department.

—— Identify a short list of candidates that match the profile requirements of each deputy minister position. Considerable emphasis should be placed on department knowledge and experience in developing short lists, which could include candidates from inside or outside the public service who have knowledge about the department or sector in question.

—— Match the skills of each candidate with the specific requirements of the department at the time of appointment (e.g., major policy change, turnaround, downsizing, reorganization or change of mandate, or consolidation).

—— Identify and develop candidates for senior deputy minister positions such as Secretary to the Cabinet, Secretary to the Treasury Board and Deputy Minister of Finance and carry out succession planning to ensure that one or two potential successors for these positions are always available.

—— Improve the transfer of responsibilities between deputy ministers by assigning prospective deputy ministers to positions that enable them to become familiar with the department before assuming their full responsibilities.

—— Ensure that the management team in the department (i.e., associate deputy minister or assistant deputy ministers) can provide the necessary support to the minister and deputy minister. For example, if the deputy minister has no previous experience in the department, it is critical that assistant deputy ministers have considerable department experience.

—— Manage centrally the career assignments of executives at the EX 4 and EX 5 levels who have been identified as having the potential to be deputy ministers. This will ensure an adequate supply of candidates from the 300 executives in this group who have the appropriate range of experience for deputy minister positions. This will require that the Public Service Commission have the capacity to manage appointments to selected developmental positions through appointment to level.

This type of career and succession planning has proved difficult in the federal public service. This is partly the result of the uncertainties that surround the appointment of deputy ministers. It also arises from the division of responsibilities between Treasury Board, the Public Service Commission and the Privy Council Office with respect to senior personnel management.[17] To develop a career and succession planning system requires constant support and reinforcement from the Prime Minister, Secretary to the Cabinet and Clerk of the Privy Council, and COSO. It requires strong staff capabilities in the three central agencies that deal with personnel management. Finally, it requires considerable co-ordination between the PCO, PSC, Treasury Board Secretariat and departments.

The Public Service Commission has been working for the past several years to improve the identification of people with high potential for executive positions, and more recently the Privy Council Office and COSO deputy ministers have been giving this area higher priority. However, more progress is required if we are to meet the requirements of the federal public service and future governments for capable deputy ministers.

9. EXECUTIVE DEVELOPMENT: The Government should act quickly on its announced intention to create a Canadian Centre for Management Development to provide training and development courses for federal government executives.

The best means of developing managers is through a career and succession planning system. However, training can also contribute to executive development.[18] The federal government has only a fair track record in providing development programs for senior executives.

To address this problem, the federal government recently announced the creation of a Canadian Centre for Management Development to provide a "credible, national, world-class centre of excellence in teaching and research in public service management". This is an important step forward. However, to establish this centre as a credible organization with a good executive development program will be a major challenge. It will require facilities, resources, expertise and a major investment in cases and other teaching materials.

Each chapter of this report illustrates some of the skills and abilities required of senior executives in government. One would expect that current executive development programs would be directed to these areas and that there would be an extensive body of literature reflecting the challenges faced by ministers, deputy ministers, and other senior public sector executives.[19] Such is not the case. Based on our research, the management development needs of government executives are as follows:

—— The Role of Senior Executives

Training on the responsibilities and accountability requirements of deputy ministers and public servants in the context of parliamentary government; the specific challenges for senior executives in the context of the Canadian Constitution and federalism; public service ethics and responsibilities; answerability requirements of public servants to Parliament; dealing with the media.

—— Support to the Minister and the Government

Instruction on how to assist ministers to develop agendas within the context of government priorities and department management requirements; how to work with ministers of state and chiefs of staff; and how to implement the minister's agenda in departments.

—— Development and Implementation of Public Policy

Developing public policies in the Canadian context; analysing and responding to external forces such as demographic change or economic upheaval; understanding how to deal with long-term problems; responding to the dynamics of the political process; the role of the media, caucus and interest groups and polls in shaping political issues and concerns; working with client groups to achieve policy or regulatory changes; developing Cabinet submissions and legislative changes; developing programs; and implementing policies and programs in departments.

—— Collective Management Responsibilities

Training about how to co-ordinate policies to support the government's agenda; manage the department-central agency interface; meet the collective management requirements of government in terms of management standards, staffing and other areas.

—— Management and Leadership in Departments

Development with respect to managing different departments; assessing the environment of a department, providing direction to departments and communicating a sense of mission and purpose to staff; downsizing and reorganizing departments; managing crises; negotiating and consulting with other departments and central agencies; providing services to the public and working with client groups, interest groups and lobby organizations; and managing regional and operational organizations.

I am very encouraged that the federal government has recognized the need for improved research into public sector management in its recent announcement concerning the Canadian Centre for Management Development. At present, the federal public service and the public sector generally have virtually no management training literature or research that deals with the development needs of executives. Little information is available that can be used to develop the skills of managers to manage in the complex environment of the federal public service. A CEO in a private company can draw on thousands of case studies; books about managing change or taking charge of an organization; [20] studies of boards of directors; and literature on leadership, succession planning, organizational design, and strategic planning in private companies. Private companies invest significant resources in training and in supporting business schools to develop such information.[21] The amount of useful information about how to manage in government is limited, and without substantial improvement in this area it will not be possible to mount an effective executive development program.

The public sector has systematically discouraged the development of such literature because of a preoccupation with the confidentiality of information. This has made it difficult for academics to conduct management research that would benefit the public service and governments. Partly for this reason, much of the academic literature has little relevance to management realities in the public service. Even though the federal government is the largest organization in Canada, it has not made a significant contribution to the development of literature with respect to public policy development or public sector management.

The Centre for Executive Development at Touraine near Ottawa has struggled to provide effective orientation programs for senior executives. It is hampered by a cost-recovery policy that results in unrealistic funding levels for the centre. The cost-recovery policy requires the centre to place too much emphasis on moving students through courses, whereas it should be developing a solid base of management knowledge with which to provide management training.

If the Government wants public service executives to be able to respond successfully to management challenges, it will have to invest more in training and the development of management literature. Public service managers will also have to make a serious commitment to training and development. The Canadian Centre for Management Development could provide the impetus and support needed to promote major improvements in public sector management research and executive development.

RECOMMENDATIONS CONCERNING PERFORMANCE ASSESSMENT FOR DEPUTY MINISTERS

10. PERFORMANCE APPRAISAL: Deputy ministers should be given more complete feedback on their performance. The Secretary to the Cabinet, through the Associate Secretary to the Cabinet for senior personnel, should discuss with each deputy minister his or her performance on an annual basis in relation to agreed upon priorities.

Performance appraisal has to be a central part of the accountability system for deputy ministers. Performance assessment is the only process that can be rigorous, comprehensive and, at the same time, sensitive to the many judgements deputy ministers are required to make.

Deputy ministers regard the current performance appraisal process as fair, but not very useful or satisfying. Generally, deputy ministers want more feedback on their objectives and their performance from the Privy Council Office. Most deputy ministers would welcome a more rigorous performance appraisal process as long as it is based on their objectives and performance with respect to supporting the minister, managing the department and achieving collective management priorities.

As emphasized in Chapter 6, the best basis for evaluating the performance of deputy ministers is to assess the quality of their judgement. Because of the unique features of each department, the priorities or working style of each minister and the challenges facing departments at various times, it is difficult to develop a single set of standards to apply to all deputy ministers. Performance assessment based on evaluating the quality of judgement can be rigorous and demanding precisely because it is aimed at providing an assessment of what deputies did in particular circumstances and whether their actions were reasonable given those circumstances. At the same time it recognizes that deputy ministers are not always the masters of their departments and that performance must be judged in the light of the various priorities, demands, constraints and opportunities facing a particular deputy minister at a given time.

The approach developed in the past few years of asking deputy ministers to write down their objectives and to discuss them with the minister is a good start. This provides the Clerk of the Privy Council, the Associate Secretary to the Cabinet, and COSO, with a basis for guidance or feedback to deputy ministers if they are pursuing a direction that could conflict with that of the Prime Minister or the Government. It also sets a benchmark against which to appraise the performance of deputy ministers. The present process, involving consultation with the minister and reports by central agencies on the deputy minister's performance, provides a good idea of the significant strengths and weaknesses of individual deputy ministers.

The size and complexity of the public service and the unique situation of each deputy minister makes it very difficult to manage an elaborate performance review process. In addition the process is time consuming for deputy ministers, COSO and the Clerk of the Privy Council. However, the performance review process can be improved by:

—— focusing the performance appraisal of deputy ministers on their judgement in providing advice and support to the minister and the Government;

—— discussing with each deputy minister his or her objectives for the department in relation to the collective management priorities of the Government;

—— reviewing the progress that deputy ministers have made in achieving their priorities given the challenges they have faced and the priorities of the minister; and

—— providing better feedback to deputy ministers with respect to their performance on an annual basis.

The management of the appraisal process will require a considerable commitment of time by the Clerk of the Privy Council and the Associate Secretary to Cabinet for Senior Personnel. The addition of an Associate Secretary of Senior Personnel who is widely respected by deputy ministers and ministers has helped the Clerk of the Privy Council make improvements in this area.

For this kind of performance appraisal process to work, the results have to be used as a basis for assigning deputy ministers. Thus, it is essential that the results of this process be conveyed to the Prime Minister when he is considering appointments, dismissals or changes of deputy ministers.

Finally, it will be necessary for the Associate Secretary to the Cabinet and his or her staff to develop a better information base regarding the individual requirements of each deputy minister job through interviews with ministers and deputy ministers and exit interviews with deputy ministers when they retire or are moved.

NOTES

CHAPTER 1

1. Such criticisms of the accountability of deputy ministers have been expressed in the following articles: Flora MacDonald, "The Minister and the Mandarins", *Policy Options*, September 1980, pp. 29-31; Lloyd Axworthy, "Control of Policy", *Policy Options*, April 1985, pp.11-14; Hugh Segal,"The Accountability of Public Servants", *Policy Options*, November 1981, pp. 11-12; and Conrad Winn, "Cabinet Control of the Public Service", *Policy Options*, March 1985,pp. 126-128.

2. It is not the purpose of this report to describe in depth the constitutional, institutional, and legal foundations of the parliamentary system of government or the functions of deputy ministers. This has already been done very well by academics in the fields of public administration and political science as well as by the Privy Council Office. The Privy Council Office has produced two excellent documents, "Responsibility in the Constitution", which was Part 1 of the "Submisssions to the Royal Commission on Financial Management and Accountability" (1979) and "The Office of the Deputy Minister" (1984) which provide a thorough and complete analysis of the foundation of the accountability system for deputy ministers. The aim of this report is to extend and complement these documents by developing insights into how this system works in practice.

3. These cases were completed by a variety of researchers. Bruce Doern from the School of Public Administration at Carleton University did five cases and provided an excellent summary report identifying some major themes from these cases. Mike Prince, who was at that time a professor of public administration at Carleton University, completed two cases. Tim Plumptre, a management consultant and author from Ottawa, contributed one case. Peter Gillespie from the Centre for Executive Development at Touraine undertook one case. Finally Reg Heasman, who was on loan from the Office of the Comptroller General, researched two cases. These cases were all done according the case methodology developed by Richard Paton. The cases were summarized in the form that appears in the report by Michael Nelson and Richard Paton.

4. Sharon Sutherland, who is a professor at the School of Public Administration, Carleton University, completed the study on the implications of parliamentary reform for public servants. This work was mostly funded by the Business Council on National Issues. See note 11 in chapter 2. Bruce Doern updated the work he did for the Lambert Commission in 1977 on the accounting officer concept in the United Kingdom.

5.   See four speeches by Gordon Osbaldeston that were produced as part of this study : "The Public Servant and Politics", *Policy Options*, January 1987, pp. 3-7; "How Deputies Are Accountable", *Policy Options*, September 1987, pp. 10-14; and "Job Description for DMs", *Policy Options*, January 1988, pp.35-37;"Dear Minister: A Letter to a Friend on Being a Successful Minister", *Policy Options*, June, 1988.

6.   Richard Paton, "The Independent Study of the Accountability of Deputy Ministers: Research Design and Methodology", National Centre for Management Research and Development Working Paper: Osbaldeston Accountability Study, London, 1988.

7.   Royal Commission on Government Organization, *Final Report*, 1962, Volume I, p. 60.

8.   Privy Council Office, "The Office of Deputy Minister", Ottawa, 1984, p. 9. See also Privy Council Office, Submission to the Royal Commission on Financial Management and Accountability, Ottawa, 1977, pp. 1-16 and 1-37.

CHAPTER 2

1.   See Privy Council Office, Submission to the Royal Commission on Financial Management and Accountability, Ottawa, 1977, pp. 1-13 to 1-16 for a discussion of the origins of collective responsibility.

2.   To understand better the challenges facing ministers assuming responsibility for a portfolio, see G.F. Osbaldeston, "Dear Minister: A Letter to an Old Friend on Being a Successful Minister", *Policy Options*, June 1988.

3.   In addition to this interview data, it is useful to note that most of the ministers who have written about their experiences as minister have not identified any major problems holding deputy ministers accountable to them. See, J. Chretien, *Straight from the Heart*, 1986, pp. 89-90; and E. Whelan, *Whelan: The Man in the Green Stetson*, 1986, pp. 155-156.

4.   See J. Hugh Faulkner, "Pressuring the Executive", *Canadian Public Administration*, Vol. 25, No. 2, (1982) for an interesting description of the role of ministers with respect to their clients.

5.   See, for example, the *Interpretation Act*, 1967-68, c. I-23.

6.   See J. Kotter, *Power and Influence: Beyond Formal Authority*, 1985, pp.18-19 and 48-50. Kotter's book is a perceptive discussion of the limitations of authority in diverse, interdependent organizations. Public sector organizations can be regarded as an extreme example of the management challenges that Kotter describes.

7.   See also, Sir Robert Armstrong, "Ministers, Politicians and Public Servants", *Public Money*, September 1985, for an excellent

description of the classic principles of ministerial responsibility and the accountability of deputy ministers to ministers in the United Kingdom.

8.   In the United Kingdom there are similar differences in the views of ministers about deputy ministers. The British Broadcasting Corporation published an excellent description of the relationships between politicians and bureaucrats in 1982. See H. Young and A. Sloaman, *No Minister*, pp. 25-26.

9.   See D. J. Savoie, "The Minister's Staff: The Need for Reform", *Canadian Public Administration*, Vol. 26, No. 4, pp. 509-524.

10.   See J. A. Chenier, "Ministers of State to Assist: Weighing the Costs and the Benefits", *Canadian Public Administration*, Vol. 28, No. 3, pp. 397-412.

11.   S.L. Sutherland and Y. Baltacioglu, "Parliamentary Reform and the Federal Public Service", Carleton University, July, 1988.

CHAPTER 3

1.   See note 1, chapter 2.

2.   See J.E. Hodgetts, *The Canadian Public Service: A Physiology of the Public Service 1867-1970*, pp. 207-208 for a discussion of the rationale for this delegation of authority to deputy ministers.

3.   See "Roles and Responsibilities of the Public Service Commission: Statutory, Delegated and Shared", Public Service Commission, April 1985, for further information on the role of PSC.

4.   See Treasury Board of Canada, "Role of the Treasury Board Secretariat and the Office of the Comptroller General", March 1983, for additional information on the responsibilities of Treasury Board.

5.   The expansion of the role of the Treasury Board in the Bennett years is explained in J.E. Hodgetts, W. McCloskey, R. Whitaker, and V.S. Wilson, *The Biography of An Institution: The Civil Service Commission of Canada 1908-1967*, 1972, pp. 137-142.

6.   See S. Sutherland and G.B. Doern, *Bureaucracy in Canada:Control and Reform*, 1985, pp. 43-80. This study provides a thorough and insightful discussion of the complex institutional framework of the federal government. It was one of the studies commissioned by the Royal Commission on the Economic Union and Development Prospects for Canada.

7.   Privy Council Office, "Submission to the Royal Commission on Financial Management and Accountability, Recent Changes in the Public Service", Part III, March 1979, p. 3-30.

8.   *Ibid*, p. 3-39.

9. *Report of the Auditor General to the House of Commons for the fiscal year ended March 31, 1983*, December 1983, Chapter 2, "Constraints to Productive Management in the Public Service". The co-authors of this report were Otto Brodtrick and Richard Paton. The overall approach to IMAA is consistent with the suggestions and recommendations presented in this chapter.

10. See *Optimum*, 1987/88, Volume 18-4, pp. 6-29 for the thoughts of three deputy ministers regarding their experience with IMAA.

11. Treasury Board of Canada, "Increased Ministerial Authority and Accountability," December 1987.

12. The accountability process proposed by IMAA closely parallels the process that the Ontario government has had in place for a few years. For a full description of the current approach of the Ontario government, see *Annual Report of the Provincial Auditor of Ontario for the fiscal year ended March 31, 1986*. IMAA is also consistent with many of the recommendations contained in the background papers to *A Study of Management and Accountability in the Government of Ontario*, which was submitted by the Canada Consulting Group Inc and Price Waterhouse Associates to the Ontario government in January, 1985.

13. For further information on the Increased Ministerial Authority and Accountability initiative, see "The IMAA Handbook: A Guide to Development and Implementation", December 10, 1987, and the decision of the Treasury Board meeting of June 30, 1986 on the subject of "Increased Authority and Accountability for Ministers and Departments", TB 800978/79/80.

CHAPTER 4

1. According to J. Kingdon the agenda setting process is the **determination of the priorities, plans or initiatives that the government and ministers consider to be most important and which require their continuing attention.** J.W. Kingdon, *Agendas, Alternatives and Public Policies*, 1984, p. 4. Kingdon provides some excellent insights into agenda setting in the United States which has some general application to Canada.

2. J. Kotter, *Power and Influence - Beyond Formal Authority*, 1985, pp. 12-51. Kotter has argued convincingly that as diversity and interdependence increase in organizations, executives have to depend on a small number of individuals and groups over whom they have no authority to achieve their agendas. To manage in this type of environment, he argues, executives in the modern era have to develop more skills and capabilities to influence various players. These basic conclusions are valid for the public sector as well, where the level of diversity and interdependence is extreme.

3. M. Nolan, "The camera never blinks in the Commons" *The Globe and Mail*, (Friday, October 16, 1987).

4.   This dynamic nature of decision making has been descibed very well by Bruce Doern and Richard Phidd in their book *Canadian Public Policy Ideas, Structure, Process*, 1983, Chapters 10 and 11.

5.   J. W. Kingdon, *op. cit.*, pp. 90-94 has illustrated that the agenda setting process in governmnet is shaped by four separate streams: problems, solutions, participants, and choice opportunities and that each of these streams has a life of its own. For example a group may pursue a particular solution unrelated to a problem. Kingdon shows the dynamic nature of agenda setting by illustrating that the execution of an agenda depends on the coupling of these various streams, policy windows and a host of factors that evolve in the course of the decision-making process.

6.   J. Galbraith, *Designing Complex Organizations*, 1973, pp. 46-53. Galbraith has demonstrated the importance of lateral relations when there is high uncertainty of information and when rules, plans and information systems are unable to cope with the uncertainity of information faced by decision-makers. This insight reinforces the notion that ministers and deputy ministers often have to develop extensive networks of contacts and continually consult with various individuals and groups to manage an agenda.

7.   See J. Pfeffer and G. R. Salancik, *The External Control of Organizations: A Resource Dependence Perspective*, 1978, p. 51. This book illustrates the importance of dependency relationships between various organizations for resources or support and their implications for the role of executives. Given that public sector organizations are heavily dependent on many different organizations, this book provides a valuable set of concepts for analysing the roles of deputy ministers.

8.   H. Kaufman, *The Administrative Behavior of Federal Bureau Chiefs*, The Brookings Institution, 1981. This study of bureau chiefs in the federal government of the United States noted that the complexity of the environment, various constraints, and the time required to deal with external demands such as congressional hearings made it very difficult to change the organization. Kaufman found that "bureau chiefs...for all the power and independence attributed to their office and for all their striving, could not make a big difference in what their organizations did during the period in which they served". p. 139.

9.   J. Kotter, *The General Managers*, 1982, pp. 59-94. Kotter's discussion of the process whereby general managers in the private sector establish an agenda, develop a network in relation to that agenda and then implement the agenda through a particular network is roughly similar to the general approach that ministers and deputy ministers use in agenda-setting.

10.   See J.D Thompson, *Organizations in Action*, 1967, pp. 132-144. Thompson has noted that the more complex, uncertain and hetrogeneous the environment the more it is necessary for the top executives to perform the boundary spanning functions that link an organization to outside groups. He also has noted that the more widely distributed the power, the more necessary it is to have an 'inner circle' that can make the judgements and compromises necessary to achieve the interests of the organization.

CHAPTER 5

1.   See "Improving Management in Government", Her Majesty's Stationary Office, United Kingdom, 1988. This report to the British Prime Minister on government structure and management found, among other matters, that "most civil servants are very conscious that senior management is dominated by people whose skills are in policy formulation and who have relatively little experience of managing or working where services are actually delivered." The most evident implication of this finding is that senior managers do not have the requisite experience to carry out their responsibilities for managing operations. In addition, the fact that more junior civil servants are very concious of the orientation of senior managers' skills would likely lead junior managers to de-emphasize development of their own managerial skills in expectation of following the "golden route to the top" through excellence in policy.

2.   This chart is adapted from some of the basic concepts explored in the organizational behaviour literature for analysing the degree of uncertainty and complexity in the environment of organizations relative to their organizational structure and functions. For example, see J.D. Thompson, *Organizations in Action*, 1967, pp. 70-82. and P.R. Lawrence and J.W. Lorsch, *Organization and Environment*, 1986, pp. 23-53. Government departments that deal frequently with major policy issues and have considerable resources are the most likely to have a complex and uncertain environment.

3.   These typical components are synthesized from elements of "Planning and Accountability Process, Employment and Immigration Canada", 3rd Edition, and "The Accountability Regime Within NR-CE", National Revenue-Customs and Excise".

4.   For a description of the current management challenges for department managers, see P.M. Tellier, "The Obligations of Public Service", Notes for Remarks to the 1988 APEX Symposium, and J.L. Manion, "New Challenges in Public Administration", The 1987 Donald Gow Memorial Lecture, Queen's University, September 25, 1987.

5.   See Chester I. Barnard, *The Functions of the Executive*, 1938, pp. 215-217.

6.   See John P. Kotter, *The Leadership Factor*, New York, 1988, pp. 9-11.

7.   B. Rawson, Deputy Minister of Western Diversification, Notes for remarks to the Association of Public Service Executives, January 1988.

8.   See Kotter's *Power and Influence: Beyond Formal Authority*, pp. 18-20.

9.   As J. Galbraith notes in *Designing Complex Organizations* pp. 51-53, the degree of uncertainty in an organization is an important consideration in design of the organization's decision processes. In addition to sensitizing officials to the minister's thinking, the "round table" meetings provide a forum for reducing uncertainty through informal lateral communication among departmental decision makers.

10.   See Henry Mintzberg, *The Nature of Managerial Work*, 1973, pp 65-75.

11.   A survey of managerial attitudes in the private and public sectors was carried out by David Zussman and Jak Jabes of the Faculty of Administration, University of Ottawa, in 1986. The findings we have noted are contained in their interim report, "Survey of Managerial Attitudes", which was distributed by the Treasury Board Secretariat to public service managers in October 1987.

12.   See James March and Herbert Simon, *Organizations*, 1958, pp. 152-153. Research on behaviour in organizations has indicated that groups often pursue their own sub-goals and ignore the overall goals of the organization. This tendency raises challenges for deputy ministers.

13.   See Patricia Day and Rudolf Klein, *Accountabilities - Five Public Services*, 1987, pp. 56-59.

14.   A useful summary of some of the approaches that have been taken in making sectoral comparisons is contained in "Public and Private Management: Are They Fundamentally Alike in All Unimportant Respects?" by Graham T. Allison, Jr., which is included in *Current Issues in Public Administration*, 1982, edited by Frederick S. Lane.

15.   A few CEOs were unwilling to accept that the definition of accountability had to be restricted to relationships where a delegation of authority had taken place (as required by the definition of accountability used for this study). These CEOs felt some degree of accountability to employees, to their customers, to market analysts, to suppliers, or to others on whom they depended for success. Nonetheless, nearly all felt a primary accountability to the board of directors, parent company, president, head office, or shareholders. This illustrates the necessity of being very clear about the obligations that one associates with one's definition of accountability.

CHAPTER 6

1.   Data on tenure of ministers and deputy ministers was gathered from three sources: A tenure survey that was completed by the Royal Commission on Financial Management and Accountability, 1979; Canadian Ministers Since Confederation, April 1987; and Privy Council Office Records. Time in office was measured as of December 31 of each year. For example, if a deputy minister was appointed on August 1, 1986, then for the year 1987 he or she would be considered to have been in office for 17 months (unless of course he or she left prior to December 31, 1987).

2.   See Minutes of Proceedings and Evidence of the Standing Committee on Public Accounts, p. 27:28, December 15, 1987.

3.   See *Passing the Baton/Managing the Process of CEO Selection*, 1987, by Richard Vancil. The process of CEO selection is compared to a relay race, where the incoming CEO and the outgoing CEO both hold the baton of power for short time as their transition takes place. This permits a smooth transfer of CEO responsibilities. Vancil shows that this common practice is made possible by corporations identifying their potential CEOs well in advance of final appointment and then grooming them for their future duties.

4.   See "Learning the Executive Alphabet", *Financial Post*, Winter 1987-88. The survey polled 1,000 Canadian CEOs.

5.   See Sir G. Vickers, *The Art of Judgement*, 1965, for an excellent discussion of the concept of judgement and the requirement for appreciative systems to guide decision-making in complex societies.

6.   Paraphrased with permission from a submission by C.R. Nixon (then Deputy Minister of National Defence) to the Lambert Commission on Financial Management and Accountability, April 24, 1978.

7.   See "Governing Values", Minister of Supply and Services Canada, 1987.

CHAPTER 7

1.   See Ontario Government, *A Study of Management and Accountability in the Government of Ontario*, The Canada Consulting Group Inc., Price Waterhouse Associates, January, 1985, Background Papers, The Accountability Structure, 8, 11-12.

2.   For an interesting discussion of this problem see remarks by the Honourable John Reid to the Association of Professional Executives (APEX) Symposium, January 21, 1988.

3.   One example of the politicization argument has been made by H. Segal, "The Accountability of Public Servants", *Policy Options*,

November 1981. For an illustration of the implications of this option for a government see H. Michelmann and J.S. Steeves, "The 1982 transition in power in Saskatchewan: the Progressive Conservatives and the public service", *Canadian Public Administration*, Spring 1985.

4.   See "The Government Managers", Report of the Twentieth Century Fund Task Force on the Senior Executive Service, Priority Press Publications, New York, 1987, pp. 8-9.

5.   The option of separate parallel accountability of public servants to parliamentary committees was recommended by the Royal Commission on Financial Management and Accountability, *Final Report*, Ottawa, 1979, pp. 374-375. It was advocated in R. Huntington and Claude-Andre Lachance, "Accountability: Closing the Loop", prepared for submission to the Special Committee on Standing Orders and Procedures", Ottawa, November 8, 1982, p.86. See also J. A. McGrath, Chairman, Report of the Special Committee on The Reform of the House of Commons, Ottawa, 1985, pp. 20-21. The McGrath Committee argues for a new doctrine of administrative responsibility for administration, which it claims is "only a slight modification of traditional parliamentary government."

6.   These conclusions parallel the findings of *A Study of Management and Accountability in the Government of Ontario*, op.cit. They recommended that "Responsibility and acccountability of the minister for total ministry performance be continued and clearly recognized, in keeping with the traditions of a parliamentary democracy.", p.12.

This report also argued that "The Public Accounts Committee and the Provincial Auditor call the attention of the government, the minister and the deputy minister to issues of managerial performance and conduct. But neither the Auditor, as a servant of the Legislature, nor the Committee is part of the internal accountability structure, and neither should have a direct role in the government's internal accountability structure", p. 21

7.   A very convincing argument is made on this point by E. Forsey and G.C. Eglington, "The Question of Confidence in Responsible Government", Report submitted to the Special Committee on the Reform of the House of Commons, 1985. Forsey and Eglington argue that there are major dangers in transferring congressional practices into the parliamentary system and that the best way to maintain the accountability of the public service to elected leaders is to ensure ministers are responsible for directing departments. This will in turn ensure that politicans keep public servants accountable to them.

8.   The option of increased accountability through central management processes and controls was advocated in various reports by the Office of the Auditor General in the late 1970s and early 1980s. See *Report of the Auditor General of Canada to the House of Commons for fiscal year ended March 31, 1979*, management controls chapter, pp. 109-132. The option was also a strong feature of the initiatives by Treasury Board Secretariat and the

Office of the Comptroller General in the early 1980s. See, for example, the Honourable Donald Johnston, President of the Treasury Board, "Accountable Management: A progress report on reforms in the management of the Government of Canada and the implementation of the recommendations of the Royal Commission on Financial Management and Accountability," 1981, pp. 10-14.

9.   For the United States see National Academy of Public Administration, "Revitalizing Federal Management: Managers and Their Overburdened Systems", November 1983, pp. 8-9. For the United Kingdom, Robin Ibbs, "Improving Management in Government: the Next Steps", Report to the Prime Minister, Her Majesty's Service, February 1988, pp. 27-28. In Canada, see *Report of the Auditor General to the House of Commons for the fiscal year ended March 31, 1983*, Chapter 2, "Constraints to Productive Management in the Public Service."

10.   The Government of the United Kingdom has produced two major statements outlining the duties of public servants. Prime Minister Thatcher announced policy guidelines for the conduct of public servants in February 1985. The guidelines are included in a statement by Sir Robert Armstrong to the Treasury and Civil Service Sub-Committee, November 27, 1985. The text of the submission to that committee by Sir Robert Armstrong is reprinted in "Ministers, Politicians and Public Servants", *Public Money*, September 1985. In addition, a supplement to those guidelines, "Duties and Responsibilities of Civil Servants", was prepared by the Cabinet Office, May 7, 1987.

11.   Privy Council Office, "The Office of the Deputy Minister", Ottawa, 1984.

12.   Privy Council Office, Submission to the Royal Commission on Financial Management and Accountability, Submission 1, Responsibility in the Constitution, Ottawa, 1977.

13.   Privy Council Office, "Notes on the Responsibilities of Public Servants in Relation to Parliamentary Committees", April 1987.

14.   See G. Osbaldeston, "Dear Minister: A letter to a friend on being a successful minister", *Policy Options*, June 1988. This speech provides an illustration of the kind of general information ministers require when taking on their responsibilities.

15.   See J. Kotter, *The General Managers*, 1982. Kotter, a Harvard Business School professor, argues after a study of general managers in the United States that "Not one of the effective executives in this study was a `professional manager'", p. 8. He also found that "extensive knowledge of the business and the organization for which one is responsible may well be essential for effective managerial decision-making under conditions of great complexity." (p. 41)

16. See R. Vancil, *Passing the Baton: Managing the Process of CEO Succession*, Boston, 1987, pp. 257-281.

17. The Office of the Auditor General recently found these institutional divisions to be a factor that inhibited career planning for the management category and that caused problems in providing leadership for human resource planning. See Office of the Auditor General, *Report of the Auditor General to the House of Commons, for the fiscal year ended March 31, 1987*, Chapter 17, Management Category, section 17.153.

18. See J. Kotter, *The Leadership Factor*, New York, 1988, pp. 12-15, 100-124, for a discussion of the current status of leadership development in private corporations and the major elements of good management development programs.

19. Kotter, *The General Managers*, p.144, argues that for management development programs to be relevant to the job of managers they have to: deal with what managers really do and why; up, down, and lateral relationships; how management differs in different settings; and why some managers are effective and why others are not. He notes throughout his book that managers operate with many intuitive as well as analytical skills and that a large degree of interpersonal relationship and network building goes with the job. All of these have to be part of management education — even though Kotter recognizes that some are not easily taught. The major development areas outlined in the report are based on the same principles that Kotter has used but they have been specifically developed for the public sector.

20. See for example, J. B. Quinn, *Strategies for Change; Logical Incrementalism*, 1980, and J. Gabarro, *The Dynamics of Taking Charge*, 1987. There are hundreds of useful books on private sector management but scarcely any in Canada that deal with public sector management.

21. See J.P. Mark, *The Empire Builders: Power, Money and Ethics Inside the Harvard Business School*, 1987, p.175.